Out of Joint and Hampstead Theatre present

The Positive Hour

By April de Angelis

faber and faber
LONDON · BOSTON

First performed at Hampstead Theatre on 27 February 1997
First performed on tour at the West Yorkshire Playhouse on 9 April 1997

Hampstead Theatre

SMART PEOPLE IN SEARCH OF AN ADVENTURE is how the 40,000 people who attend Hampstead Theatre each year have been described. The adventure they are pursuing is the discovery of new plays by both the country's undiscovered and most prestigious playwrighting talent.

Past successes have included Terry Johnson's DEAD FUNNY which enjoyed not one but two successful West End productions and three national tours, OUTSIDE EDGE (now a popular television series), many plays by Mike Leigh, BURN THIS with John Malkovich and Juliet Stevenson, Philip Ridley's THE FASTEST CLOCK IN THE UNIVERSE and GHOST FROM A PERFECT PLACE and three plays by Frank McGuinness, including SOMEONE WHO'LL WATCH OVER ME with Stephen Rea and Alec McCowan. Most recent successes include SWEET PANIC by film and television writer Stephen Poliakoff, with Harriet Walter and Saskia Reeves, SOME SUNNY DAY by Martin Sherman starring Rupert Everett and Corin Redgrave, THE MEMORY OF WATER, a poignant and funny first play by Shelagh Stephenson, which will be seen on tour later this year, and THE ELEVENTH COMMANDMENT by stand-up comedian David Schneider.

A theatrical power house and much more...

"At what other serious theatre can you drop in for a do-it yourself cup of tea and natter? And where do cast and audience booze more comfortably together after the show? Nowhere is a happy full house more gratifying than at Hampstead." Mike Leigh

By becoming a member of Hampstead Theatre you will receive advance information on Hampstead Theatre productions, in the West End and on tour, as well as discounts on tickets. Contact the Box Office on 0171 722 9301.

Hampstead Theatre

Swiss Cottage, 98 Avenue Road, London NW3 3EX
Box Office: 0171 722 9301

Hampstead Theatre Ltd is a registered charity and is funded by The London Arts Board,
The London Borough of Camden and The London Borough Grants Scheme. We are
grateful to the National Lottery, through the Arts Council of England, for an award
towards a feasibility study for a new theatre at Swiss Cottage, so that more people can
see more shows.

Out of Joint was founded by Max Stafford-Clark and Sonia Friedman in 1993. Max Stafford-Clark comes to Out of Joint from The Royal Court Theatre where he was Artistic Director from 1979 to 1993. Prior to this he founded Joint Stock Theatre Group with William Gaskill and Out of Joint's name celebrates this link.

The company's aim is to generate and produce new writing for the stage and to tour this work both nationally and internationally. On occasion a classic has been paired with a new play and both have been performed in repertoire.

Out of Joint's first production was Sue Townsend's *The Queen And I* which toured and played in the West End before touring Australia extensively earlier last year. Stephen Jeffreys' new play on the life of the Restoration rake and poet the Earl of Rochester, was called *The Libertine* and played with a revival of the Restoration classic by Etherege, *The Man of Mode*. Last year Timberlake Wertenbaker wrote *The Break of Day* which was produced in repertoire with Chekhov's *Three Sisters*. *Three Sisters* played a memorable season in promenade at Rossway Park, a large country house outside London.

The Steward of Christendom won much praise for Sebastian Barry, Donal McCann and the company. It ran for two seasons at both The Royal Court Theatre in London and The Gate Theatre in Dublin. Internationally it played to acclaim in Luxembourg, Australia and New Zealand, and has recently completed a triumphant season in New York.

Donal McCann in
The Steward of Christendom
photo: John Haynes

Out of Joint's most recent production, *Shopping And Fucking*, began life at The Royal Court in September 1996. It has already toured England, become a focus of national interest and been revived in the West End. Later this year it will play in Italy, Australia, New Zealand and Israel.

Antony Ryding in *Shopping And Fucking*
photo: John Haynes

Out of Joint consistently champions the work of contemporary writers, whether they are well-known names such as Sue Townsend or newcomers like Mark Ravenhill, whose first play has been such a phenomenal success. In just three years the company has presented an astonishing variety of work and has established itself as a powerful new voice in British theatre.

Out of Joint's past productions:
The Queen And I: Sue Townsend
Road: Jim Cartwright
The Libertine: Stephen Jeffreys
The Man of Mode: George Etherege
The Steward of Christendom: Sebastian Barry
Three Sisters: Anton Chekhov, new translation by Stephen Mulrine
The Break of Day: Timberlake Wertenbaker
Shopping And Fucking: Mark Ravenhill
The Positive Hour: April de Angelis

Out of Joint's future production plans include a co-production with the Royal Court of *Blue Heart* by Caryl Churchill which will premiere at The Traverse Theatre, Edinburgh, prior to a national and international tour.

FREE MAILING LIST
To stay fully informed, join Out of Joint's mailing list by sending your name, address and postcode to the address below.

20-24 Eden Grove, London N7 8ED Tel: 0171 609 0207
Fax: 0171 609 0203   email: ojo@outofjoint.demon.co.uk

Between 1994 and 1997, Out of Joint has played in the following towns and cities, many of them several times:

Adelaide Festival Centre, Australia

Gold Coast, Australia

Melbourne, Australia

Monash, Australia

Newcastle, Australia

Sydney Festival, Australia

Theatre Royal, Bath

Rossway Park, Berkhamsted

Grand Theatre, Blackpool

South Hill Park, Bracknell

Gardner Arts Centre, Brighton

Theatre Royal, Brighton

Old Vic, Bristol

Theatre Royal, Bury St Edmunds

Arts Theatre, Cambridge

Marlowe Theatre, Canterbury

New Theatre, Cardiff

Warwick Arts Centre, Coventry

Festival Theatre, Chichester

Hawth, Crawley

Civic Theatre, Darlington

Gate Theatre, Dublin

Lyric Theatre, Hammersmith

Hampstead Theatre

New Theatre, Hull

Madras, India

Calcutta, India

Delhi, India

Bombay, India

Nuffield, Lancaster

West Yorkshire Playhouse, Leeds

Haymarket Theatre, Leicester

Everyman Theatre, Liverpool

Royal Court Theatre, London

Vaudeville Theatre, London

Theatre des Capucins, Luxembourg

Maly Theatre, Moscow

Corn Exchange, Newbury

Newcastle Playhouse

BAM, New York

Theatre Royal, Norwich

Playhouse Theatre, Oxford

The Arts Centre, Poole

Harlequin, Redhill

Palace, Watford

New Zealand Festival, Wellington

New Victoria Theatre, Woking

Connaught Theatre, Worthing

THE POSITIVE HOUR:

27 February - 5 April Hampstead Theatre
Box Office 0171 722 9301

9 - 19 April West Yorkshire Playhouse
Box Office 0113 244 2111

22 - 26 April Cambridge Arts Theatre
Box Office 01223 503333

29 April - 3 May Everyman Theatre, Liverpool
Box Office 0151 709 4776

7 - 10 May Warwick Arts Centre, Coventry
Box Office 01203 524524

13 - 17 May Palace Theatre, Watford
Box Office 01923 225671

21 - 24 May Newcastle Playhouse
Box Office 0191 230 5151

The Positive Hour

By April de Angelis

Cast in alphabetical order

Nicola	Kate Ashfield
Paula	Julia Lane
Miranda	Margot Leicester
Emma	Patti Love
The Man	David Sibley
Roger	Robin Soans
Victoria	Holly Searson
	or Kitty Stafford-Clark

Director	Max Stafford-Clark
Designer	Julian McGowan
Lighting Designer	Johanna Town
Sound	Scott Myers

Assistant Director	Shabnam Shabazi
Voice Coach	Julia Wilson-Dixon
Set constructed by	Scott Fleary
Set painted by	Paddy Hamilton
Production Photographer	John Haynes
Projection Photographer	John Turner
Projection models	Mark Livesey & Ros Coombes
Hair	Judy Flynn
Programme cover	Dewynters & Iain Lanyon

FOR HAMPSTEAD THEATRE

Production Manager	John Titcombe
Company Stage Manager	Jane Erridge
Deputy Stage Manager	Julie Issott
Assistant Stage Manager	Suzanne Bourke
Deputy Technical Manager	Philip Gladwell
Wardrobe Supervisor	Patricia Budden

FOR OUT OF JOINT

Production & Company Manager	Rob Young
Deputy Stage Manager	Helen Barratt

with special thanks to the Royal National Theatre Studio who funded Out Of Joint's workshop for THE POSITIVE HOUR in June 1996.

Out of Joint and Hampstead Theatre would like to thank the following for their help with this production:

computer props supplied by Apple Computer UK Ltd; radiator supplied by Willesden Green Architectural Salvage 0181 459 2947; school books supplied by Letts Educational; mobile phone supplied by The Carphone Warehouse

THE POSITIVE HOUR was originally commissioned by the Royal Court Theatre

APRIL DE ANGELIS (Author)

April is currently under commission to Out of Joint and the RSC. Previous plays include *Playhouse Creatures* (Sphinx Theatre Company) which is being revived at The Old Vic later this year, and *Hush* (Royal Court) which was also directed by Max Stafford-Clark. Other plays include: *Soft Vengeance* (Graeae Theatre Company); *The Life and Times of Fanny Hill* (adaptation of James Cleland novel for Red Shift); *Ironmistress* (ReSisters Theatre Co). Radio includes: *Visitants* (Radio 4) and *The Outlander* (Radio 5) which won the Writer's Guild Award, 1992. April wrote the libretto for Jonathan Dove's new Opera *Flight* for Glyndebourne 1998. For television: *Aristophanes*.

KATE ASHFIELD (Nicola)

Most recently *Shopping and Fucking* and *The Break of Day* (Out of Joint/Royal Court) and *Three Sisters* (Out of Joint). For Hampstead Theatre *Bearing Fruit* and *A Collier's Friday Night*. Other theatre includes: *Peaches* and *Blasted* (Royal Court) and *The Importance of Being Earnest* (Royal Exchange) . Television credits include *Prime Suspect, Fist of Fun, Seed , No Bananas* and recently *Soldier, Soldier*. For film: *Princess Caraboo*.

JULIA LANE (Paula)

For Hampstead Theatre, *Gaucho* and *The Fancy Man*. Other theatre includes *The Homecoming* (Haymarket Theatre, Leicester); *And All Because the Lady Loves* (Cockpit Theatre); *Jane Eyre* (Birmingham Repertory Theatre); *The Changeling, Macbeth, the Snowman* (Contact Theatre); *Shylock* (Riverside) and *Abolition* (Plaines Plough/Bristol Old Vic). Television credits include *Prime Suspect, Jake's Progress, Thieftakers, Harry Enfield & Chums, Heartbeat, Brighton Belles, A Pinch of Snuff, Floodtide, Inspector Morse, Capital City, Sharp End, Jute City, Boon, Achilles Heel* and *Casualty*. Film credits: *Black Eyes, Woman at War, Memories of Midnight* and *Secret Rapture*.

MARGOT LEICESTER (Miranda)

Theatre includes *Broken Glass* (Royal National Theatre and West End) for which she was nominated for an Olivier Award; *Les Liaisons Dangereuses, The Last Yankee, An Enemy of the People, Antony and Cleopatra* and *Taming of the Shrew* (all West End); *Measure for Measure, The Crucible* and *Macbeth* (all directed by David Thacker for Young Vic); *Duet for One* and *A Street Car Named Desire* (Dukes Playhouse, Lancaster) *Merchant of Venice, Uncle Vanya, Bingo* (Library Theatre, Manchester) and repertory seasons at Exeter, Coventry, Birmingham and Sheffield. Television credits currently include *Peak Practice, Where the Heart is* (to be seen in March) and *Broken Glass*. Other television includes *King Girl, Hetty Wainthropp Investigates, Casualty, Killing Me Softly, Ghosts, Measure for Measure, The Bill, Heartbeat, Medics, Chandler & Co, Families* and *Perfect Scoundrels*.

PATTI LOVE (Emma)

Patti Love is returning to Hampstead Theatre, where she previously appeared in *The Black and White Minstrels* by C P Taylor, *Union Jack and The Bonzo Dog* by Stanley Eveling. Other numerous theatre credits include, most recently a national tour of *The Provok'd Wife* directed by Stuart Burge and *Lysistrata* for the Peter Hall Company in the West End. Productions for the Royal Court include *Mary Barnes* by David Edgar and *Masterpieces* by Sarah Daniels; under Max Stafford-Clark's direction she appeared in *Serious Money* by Caryl Churchill, *Three Birds Alighting on a Field* by Timberlake Wertenbaker and *All Things Nice* by Sharman MacDonald. She has worked for the RSC, including *Henry IV Parts I & II* and for the RNT *Uncle Vanya* and *The Spanish Tragedy*.
She wrote and performed her own one woman show *Colette*, based on the life of the writer Colette. Films include *That'll Be The Day, The Krays, A Long Good Friday, An Awfully Big Adventure* for Mike Newell and *Steaming* directed by Joseph Losey. Television includes *Middlemarch, Escape from Sobibor, Casualty* and most recently *Moll Flanders*.

JULIAN MCGOWAN (Design)

Theatre designs include: *The Steward of Christendom* (for Out of Joint at the Brooklyn Academy of Music, New York) *Three Sisters* (Out of Joint); *Shopping and Fucking* and *The Break of Day* (Out of Joint/Royal Court); *Translations* (Abbey Theatre, Dublin); *Old Times* (Wyndhams Theatre, West End); *Venice Preserved; The Possibilites; The LA*

Plays (Almeida); *Don Juan* (Royal Exchange); *Heart Throb* (Bush); *Princess Ivona* (ATC); *Doctor of Honour* (Cheek by Jowl); *Prin* (Lyric Hammersmith/West End); *The Tempest, Romeo and Juliet, Pericles* (Oxford Stage Co.); *The Rivals, Man and Superman, The Playboy of the Western World, Hedda Gabler* (Glasgow Citizens'); *Imagine Drowning* (Hampstead) and *The Lodger* (Hampstead/Royal Exchange); *Hamlet* and *Total Eclipse* (Greenwich); *Tess of the d'Urbervilles* (West Yorkshire Playhouse); *The Changeling, The Wives' Excuse* (RSC); *A Doll's House* (Theatr Clwyd); *Torquatto Tasso* (Edinburgh Festival); *Downfall, Blood, American Bagpipes, The Treatment* (Royal Court/Greenwich Theatre). Opera includes: *Cosi fan tutte* (New Israeli Opera); *Eugene Onegin* (Scottish Opera); *The Nightingale and the Rose* and *Siren Song* (Almeida Opera Festival).

SCOTT MYERS (Sound)

Studied theatre lighting and sound with Len Coutu, an ex French Resistance operative and old-timer from the golden age of Broadway. Scott began designing sound for theatre in 1969 on a production of Ionesco's *The Sofa*. Since then the list of credits has grown to include almost the entire repertoire of schlock American musicals and nearly every Neil Simon play. He spent six years in Hollywood as a sound recordist on such memorable films as *They Only Come Out at Night* and *The Steven Weed Story*. UK sound design credits include: *Richard III, The Madness of King George, Arcadia, Racing Demon* (Royal National Theatre) *Arcadia* and *Racing Demon* also on Broadway; *In the Company of Men* (Royal Shakespeare Company); and *The Glass Menagerie, Arcadia* and *A Doll's House* (West End).

HOLLY SEARSON (Victoria)

Holly goes to The Emmanuel School, Mill Hill. Her photographic work includes Pippa Dee, Tomy, Boots and J D Williams. This is Holly's first stage appearance.

SHABNAM SHABAZI
(Assistant Director)

Shabnam has commissioned and directed many new plays, most recently: *Tonguetied* by Sara Clifford (Young Vic Studio); *Three Tides Turning* by Louise Warren (Finborough); *Northern Lights* by Clare Bayley (New Grove).

She has worked as director and workshop leader for many theatres and touring companies in London and across England. She was resident Assistant Director at Paines Plough and Literary Manager of the London New Play Festival.

She is currently Education Officer at Theatre Centre, Britain's first established Young People's touring theatre company. She is also a Drama Adviser for the Arts Council of England.

Forthcoming productions include a new play by Clare Bayley (ACE commission); a site specific project by Nick Sutton and an Education Project in collaboration with Sibiu International Theatre Festival, Romania.

DAVID SIBLEY (The Man)

Theatre includes *Lion in the Streets* (Hampstead Theatre); *The Marriage of Mr Mississippi* (New End Theatre); *Hamlet* (Royal Court); *Arturo Ui* (Half Moon); *Cocks & Hens* (Soho Poly); *The Last Elephant* and *Turning Over* (Bush Theatre); *A Month in the Country* (Palace Theatre, Watford); *Ripped* (The Cockpit Theatre); *The Great Highway* (The Gate Theatre); *Taming of the Shrew, Romeo and Juliet* (Chester Gateway); *Playboy of the Western World* and *Much Ado About Nothing* (Exeter, Northcott). For television *Drovers Gold, Frontiers, The Manageress, Middlemarch, Annie's Bar, The Bill, In Suspicious Circumstances, The Big One, Casualty, Inspector Alleyn, Young Indy, Redemption, Minder, Traitors, Talking Takes Two, The Nightmare Years, Prisoners of Childhood, Wilderness Road, An Inspector Calls, The Kitchen* and *The Fatal Spring*. Film credits include *Incognito, Princess Cariboo, Willow, Hinterland, Ultimate City, Man from a Far Country, Ghandi* and *Yanks*.

ROBIN SOANS (Roger)

Most recently in *Shopping and Fucking* for Out of Joint/Royal Court. Other theatre includes *Waiting Room Germany, Three Birds Alighting on a Field, Star-Gazie Pie & Sauerkraut* and *Etta Jenks* (Royal Court); *Volpone* (Royal National Theatre); *Raising Fires* (Bush); *The Country Wife, Venetian Twins* and *Murder in the Cathedral* (Royal Shakespeare Company); *Walpurgis Night, Gringo Planet* (The Gate Theatre); *Germinal, Berlin Days - Hollywood Nights* (The Place & tour); *Bete Noir* (Young Vic);

Fashion (Leicester Haymarket/Tricycle); *Thatcher's Women* (Tricycle & tour); *The Rivals* (Nottingham Playhouse); *A Prick Song for the New Leviathan* (Old Red Lion); *The Shaming of Bright Millar* (Contact Theatre); *Queer Fish* (BAC); *The Worlds, Hamlet, Woyzec, Chobham Amour* (Half Moon) and *The Strongest Man in the World* (Roundhouse). Most recently for television *Rebecca* and *Jonathon Creek*. Other credits include: *Casualty, The Marshall and the Madwoman, Inspector Alleyn, Anna Lee, Lovejoy, The Specials, This Land of England, The Last Place on Earth, The Chelworth Inheritance, Bergerac, Lord Peter Wimsey, The Bill, Tales of Sherwood Forest, Bard on the Box*. Films include: *Comrades, Absolution, The Patricia Neal Sotry, Hidden City, Blue Juice* and *Clockwork Mice*.

KITTY STAFFORD-CLARK
(Victoria)

Kitty is eight years old. She moved to Northbridge House School two years ago and has performed there in *The Pirates of Penzance*. She likes Maths, Science and Nature and she loves Alfredo and Lily the cats. She went to India last year to see Out of Joint's production of *Three Sisters*, her favourite actors were Barney and Jenna.

MAX STAFFORD-CLARK
(Director)

Founded Joint Stock Theatre group in 1974 following his Artistic Directorship of The Traverse Theatre, Edinburgh. From 1979 to 1993 he was Artistic Director of The Royal Court Theatre. In 1993 he founded his touring company, Out of Joint, and he is currently an Associate Director of The Royal Court Theatre. His work as a Director has overwhelmingly been with new writing, and he has commissioned and directed first productions by many of the country's leading writers. These include: *Fanshen, The Speakers* (both with William Gaskill), *Light Shining In Buckinghamshire* and *Cloud Nine* for Joint Stock; *The Arbor, Operation Bad Apple, Top Girls, Rita Sue And Bob Too, Falkland Sound, Tom And Viv, Rat In The Skull, Aunt Dan And Lemon, Serious Money, Our Country's Good, Icecream, My Heart's A Suitcase, Hush* and *Three Birds Alighting On A Field* for the Royal Court; *The Queen And I, The Libertine, The Steward of Christendom,*

The Break of Day and *Shopping and Fucking* for Out of Joint. In addition he has directed *The Seagull, The Pope's Wedding, The Recruiting Officer* and *King Lear* for the Royal Court; *A Jovial Crew, The Country Wife* and *The Wives Excuse* for The Royal Shakespeare Company; and *Road, The Man of Mode* and *Three Sisters* for Out of Joint. He has also directed for The Abbey Theatre, Dublin and Joseph Papp's Public Theatre, New York. He has been visiting Professor of Drama at Royal Holloway and Bedford College, The Masie Glass Professor of Drama at Sheffield University and he is an Honorary Fellow of Rose Bruford College. His book *Letters to George* was published in 1989.

JOHANNA TOWN
(Lighting Design)

Theatre credits include: *The Steward of Christendom* and *Road* (Out of Joint - Royal Court, Dublin, Sydney, New York); *Three Sisters, Shopping and Fucking, Road, The Break of Day* (Out of Joint): *Beautiful Thing* (Duke of York's & The Bush) *Charlie's Aunt* (Watford); *The Lodger* (Hampstead & Royal Exchange); *Richard II, Street Captives, The Misfits* (Royal Exchange): *Disappeared* (Leicester Haymarket); *Salvation, The Snow Orchid* (London Gay Theatre); *The Set-Up, Crackwalker* (Gate Theatre); *Celestina* (ATC); *Josephine* (BAC); designs for the Royal Court Theatre include: *Harry & Me, The Kitchen, Faith Healer, Babies, The Editing Process, Hush, Pale Horse, Peaches, Search & Destroy, Women Laughing, Talking in Tongues*. Three seasons with the Liverpool Playhouse including: *Macbeth, The Beaux Strategm, Madame Mao*.
Opera credits include: *Otello, The Magic Flute* (Opera du Nice): *La Traviata , The Magic Flute* (MTL, Donmar, Hamburg, Holland); *The Marriage of Figaro, Eugene Onegin, The Abduction from the Seraglio* (Opera 80).
Johanna is currently Head of Lighting for the Royal Court Theatre.

"Because I do not hope to know again
The infirm glory of the positive hour"

T S ELIOT

The Positive Hour

First published in 1997
by Faber and Faber Limited
3 Queen Square London WC1N 3AU

Typeset by Faber and Faber Ltd
Printed in England by Mackays of Chatham plc, Chatham, Kent

April de Angelis is hereby identified as author of this
work in accordance with Section 77 of the Copyright,
Designs and Patents Act 1988

All rights whatsoever in this work are strictly reserved. Applications for permission for any use whatsoever including performance rights must be made
in advance, prior to any such proposed use, to Casarotto Ramsay Limited,
National House, 60–66 Wardour Street, London W1V 4ND. No performance
may be given unless a licence has first been obtained.

A CIP record for this book
is available from the British Library

ISBN 0–571–19139–8

2 4 6 8 10 9 7 5 3 1

Act One

SCENE ONE

Miranda's office. Miranda sits at her desk. Paula enters.

Paula I don't want any more bollocks.

Miranda Pardon?

Paula Bollocks.

Miranda Now, Paula . . .

Paula I'm a desperate woman. You must've seen one of us before? We smoke and have hastily applied mascara. It's my daughter. Victoria Savage. Eight and three-quarters. Her favourite groups are Spice Girls and Michael Jackson. I haven't got the heart to tell her he's a pervert. I mean, children are in their own special world, aren't they?

Miranda I've got your file here.

Paula Temporarily fostered with the Clements. Mr and Mrs Patrick of Sussex. They don't like me going there. They say it upsets Victoria. Course it does. I'm her mother. It's a wrench when I leave. She cries, I cry. It's a fucking mess. Patrick's a bank manager and Isobel doesn't know what to do with herself. They have a mug tree. Know the sort? Victoria's a very demanding child. That house was dead and now they're wetting themselves with having a bit of life in their life, but it's my fucking bit of life.

Miranda Paula, fostering is a temporary arrangement and every effort is made to return the child to its mother.

Paula So they say.

Miranda This is my first morning, Paula. You probably know that I've been away for a bit. I just wanted the opportunity to meet you and to discuss your situation.

Paula You see, this thing has happened in their heads. Somehow they think they are Victoria's parents and I am a passing annoyance.

Miranda I'm sure that's not the case.

Paula And people are going to look at them and look at me and think she's better off with them. But she's my daughter.

Miranda A child is always better off with its mother unless there are serious concerns for its welfare.

Paula Do you like me?

Miranda I haven't introduced myself. Miranda Hurst.

Paula Because it's important, isn't it, Miranda, that you like me? What you think is important?

Miranda My assessment will have a bearing on the outcome of your case, but it would be bad practice if I let personal opinion interfere with professional judgement.

Paula So what are you going to do about Victoria?

Miranda Well, there's nothing I can do today.

Paula No one's listening to me.

Miranda Of course we want to place your daughter back with you. That's terribly important, but what we have to do is to see that as a goal at the end of a longer term process.

Paula A process?

Miranda Yes.

Paula Five months now they've had her.

Miranda Yes, Paula.

Paula So how long's a process?

Miranda It's as long as it takes.

Paula I'm sick of people keep putting me off.

Miranda Paula . . .

Paula Don't fucking Paula me. (*She pulls a razor blade out of her bag and holds it to her wrist.*) Don't even fucking move.

Miranda Please, Paula, put that away.

Paula I'm never happy, not without Victoria. I wake up in the morning and it's like there's a big hole in my chest only I'm too scared to look down because once I do I'm going to feel this pain.

Miranda It must be very hard. Now, please, let's be calm.

Paula No. Let's be hysterical. Let's have blood.

Miranda Of course we must start the whole thing moving now.

Paula Moving, that's good, Miranda.

Miranda Because, believe me, I want your daughter to be given back to you very much. The problems are solvable. I will have failed if we don't get Victoria back with you and I don't want to fail. Why don't you sit down and put that away and then we can begin.

Pause. Paula sits down and places the blade near to her on the desk between them.

Paula I'm putting it here.

3

Miranda Actually I had a sort of collapse. An exhaustion thing. After six months my doctor said, 'Yes, go back to work, but avoid stressful situations.' This is my first day.

Paula Oh. Sorry.

Miranda opens Paula's file.

Miranda We think it was a virus.

Paula There's a lot of weird things about.

Miranda Well. I'd just like to go over a few details to start with. Accommodation, has anything changed?

Paula No.

Miranda You're still in a bedsit?

Paula I'm on the council waiting-list. Lewisham.

Miranda I'll try giving them a ring. See if we can get any movement on that. You're claiming supplementary benefit?

Paula Yes.

Miranda Are you looking for work?

Paula No.

Miranda I think it's important not to become defeated.

Paula looks blank.

Work is a stabilizer. It's also one way out of bedsit land. That would be a plus for Victoria living with you again. Having a criminal record doesn't mean that you're unemployable.

Paula Doesn't help though, does it, Miranda? Do one stupid thing and it follows you for life. I stole a poxy video cassette recorder. Three months in Holloway. That's how I lost Victoria.

4

Miranda And Michael?

Paula Michael?

Miranda Victoria told the Clements that she was scared of Michael.

Paula That must be from when I broke my arm. I told them it was an accident.

Miranda How did that happen?

Paula I broke it and she thought he broke it but she was mixed up. Kids do get mixed up. Have you got kids?

Miranda No. Victoria says he broke it and she's frightened he'll break her arm.

Paula It was an accident.

Miranda How often does he hit you?

Paula The arm was a one-off thing. He's never hit her.

Miranda She just has to watch him hitting you. Does he live with you?

Paula On and off.

Miranda It doesn't sound like a very sustaining relationship.

Paula He's my boyfriend. I'm not like a punch bag. It's not like that. Just when we have fights.

Miranda There's never an excuse for a man to hit a woman.

Paula The longer they have Victoria the less likely it is I'll get her back.

Miranda That's not true.

Paula Fuck off, it is. She's my daughter. Sometimes I

5

wake up and I lie there and I can't get up. I can't think of a reason to get up.

Miranda But at the same time there are positive steps you can take, Paula. You could decide to leave a violent man. Do things that are in your power first.

Paula I love him though.

Miranda It's a question of priorities, isn't it?

Paula It would help, if I got rid of him.

Miranda Absolutely. Anything that demonstrates your desire to provide a good home for your daughter. And wouldn't it be a positive step for you?

Paula Do you think I'll be able to leave him?

Miranda Yes. I do. I've often found people have a great deal more in them than they realize.

SCENE TWO

Emma in a stranger's flat. She looks about her.

Emma How long have you been in banking? (*Pause.*) I think it's fascinating what you were saying about index linking. (*Pause.*) I feel a bit light-headed actually. I shouldn't drink on an empty stomach but I always do. It's stupid because the next morning you pay for it. (*Pause.*) This is the sort of thing you're always told not to do. Going back to a stranger's house. But then how do you get to know someone if you don't see their home? You get to know them a lot quicker than if you were just sitting in a pub. You've got pictures on the wall. I like pictures. (*She looks at them.*) Is that a Tillier? He's marvellous, isn't he? With him a smudge isn't a smudge, is it? It's movement. So have you ever used one of these agencies before?

(*Pause.*) I used to think it was a degrading idea. An agency. That only social misfits used them. Which of course is totally untrue. I mean, look at us. (*Pause.*) What are you up to in there?

The door opens and a man enters. He is naked from the waist up and he wears a black hood, studded collar and belt.

Oh my God. (*Pause.*) I think you've got the wrong idea about me. Absolutely and utterly the wrong idea. I have to go now. (*She grabs her stuff.*) I'm not like that. I just wanted to talk.

Hooded Man Okay.

He sits down. Emma heads to the door. Stops.

Emma I really am not into that. I'm a feminist and a pacifist. I've never hurt anyone in my life.

Hooded Man Of course.

Emma You seemed nice. But that's the thing with men – you can never tell. It's the same as with my ex-husband. One day he just turned round and said, 'We've grown apart.' Just like that.

Hooded Man Very upsetting.

Emma Devastating.

Hooded Man Absolutely.

Pause.

Emma I can hear a dog barking somewhere. I thought about getting a dog when Alan left but then I couldn't bear the idea of all that hair on the cushions. Pit-bulls are becoming very common. Three kids and a pit-bull. In working-class families. You know, the revolutionary masses. Alan was a Trotskyist for years but then it sort of

7

wore off. About the time the housing market went through the roof. Now he's got a restaurant. For the last three years of our marriage he didn't want sex, he just wanted to do the menus.

Hooded Man You talk a lot.

Emma Is there anything wrong with that?

Hooded Man No. It was a comment. Hit me.

Emma What?

Hooded Man gives her a long black glove.

Hooded Man On the legs. With that.

Emma This is absolutely ridiculous.

Hooded Man Go on.

Pause. Emma takes the gloves and hits him.

Hooded Man Thank you.

Emma This really isn't me. (*She makes to exit.*)

Hooded Man Don't go.

Emma I'm sorry. I'm normal. (*She exits quickly.*)

SCENE THREE

Paula and Miranda. Miranda's office.

Paula Well, I did it. This is how I did it. I drank neat vodka. Then I taped a note to my door which said, 'It's over, love Paula.' Then I left his reproduction Armani underpants in a plastic bag on the mat. Then I hid. Mastermind. Only I never closed my window. 2 a.m., I wake up and he's looming over me. 'Fuck you, Paula,' he said. 'Fuck you, Michael,' I said. That went on for a bit. I said, 'I'm sorry, Michael, but what can I do? I have to demonstrate my desire to provide a good home for my daughter.' He tried snogging. It didn't work. Well, it did for about two minutes. But, anyway. Cut to me an hour later. More vodka had been swilled. More tears had watered the ashtray. I was doing it. I didn't even know why I was doing it. Finally, I took the taped note off the door and stuck it on my forehead. I said, 'Michael, it's not that I don't think you're a decent bloke underneath, but who's got a spade big enough to shovel off all the shit?' (*She turns slightly to one side.*) That's how I got my eye. This morning I woke up and I swear I felt like Bambi. I lay there for a bit just listening to the sounds coming in the window and I thought, this is nice.

Miranda I think that was a very sensible move to make.

Paula Sensible? How about fucking huge?

Miranda Well, let's just see how things go.

Paula How do you mean?

Miranda Over the next month or so.

Paula The next month?

Miranda See how things pan out.

Paula Another month?

Miranda That's only reasonable. Don't you think?

Paula What about the rest of it? My flat?

Miranda I'm waiting for Lewisham housing to phone me back.

Paula Don't hold your breath. I have to have something, Miranda. I can't stay in that room with less than I had before. Do you know?

Miranda Have you thought any more about work?

Paula No.

Miranda There's a sense of self to be found in work, Paula. It can mean more than just economic independence. I don't want to force anything on you. What I'd like ideally is for us to be in a kind of partnership. Working on your situation together. Both contributing.

Paula I just want Victoria back.

Miranda I can't just give her back to you. You know that. (*Pause.*) I think this is an opportunity for you, Paula. To do more than just get back what you've lost. To imagine better for yourself and go for it. Perhaps the issue here is retraining of some sort. I have a client who is taking a GCSE.

Paula A what?

Miranda A GCSE. In ancient history. The Romans fascinated her. Apparently they had central-heating systems.

Paula Lucky bastards. What does she want to be, a central-heating engineer?

Miranda No.

Paula A centurion?

Miranda I should think that would be difficult. Was there a subject that particularly interested you at school?

Paula No.

Miranda Well, how do you see your future?

Paula I could meet a rich man. I could win the lottery.

Miranda That's a bit of a gamble.

Paula It's better than nothing.

Miranda I think it is pretty much nothing, don't you?

The job centre could give you retraining information. We could discuss it together. Will you think about it?

Paula All right.

Miranda I think you could build a real future for yourself, Paula. Don't you?

Paula Miranda, can I ask you a favour? I'm visiting Victoria at the weekend. I haven't got the train fare. Twenty quid. Is there any chance of me borrowing it?

Miranda Yes, all right. (*Gives Paula money.*)

Paula Thanks, partner. (*She begins to go.*)

Miranda I'm starting a small group, Paula. Just a few of us. We'd meet regularly. Starting Tuesday. A sort of support group. We'd share advice. Discuss our feelings.

Paula What for?

Miranda I think it's a creative way to work. Are you interested?

Paula No thanks. That sort of thing makes me feel nauseous. (*She goes to exit again.*)

Miranda It would look like you're making an effort, wouldn't it? Taking some control. You might even enjoy it.

Paula hesitates momentarily before she exits. Miranda, who has taken her coat, hurries out.

SCENE FOUR

The group meets. A semi-circle of chairs. Nicola sits holding her bag. Paula enters.

Paula Is this the group?

Nicola What?

Paula The group?

Nicola Oh, the group. Yes, yes, it is.

Paula Right. You're not exactly what I'd have called a group.

Nicola My name's Nicola.

Paula Paula.

Nicola You can call me Nick or Nicky. Or Nicola.

Paula Right.

Pause.

Nicola Soon we won't be nervous. After a couple of meetings our nerves will wear off. Then we won't be able to remember what it was like to feel . . . nervous.

Paula What's in that bag, Nicky?

Nicola My bag?

Paula 'Cos if it's alive you'll have squeezed all the juices out of it by now.

Nicola It's just books. I take them out with me because I don't like leaving them at home.

Paula Why's that?

Nicola It's just a feeling.

Paula It's lucky you don't feel that way about the chairs.

Nicola Oh, no. That would be mad.

Paula Yes. What sort of group is this, anyway?

Nicola A woman's group.

Paula Fuck. Is it?

12

Nicola Miranda must have mentioned it.

Paula I must have suppressed it. Are you a client of Miranda's?

Nicola Off and on. We keep in touch. We thought it might be a good idea if I came along. I think it's a positive thing for women to meet in this way. To share and empower. I was in two groups before. (*Pause.*) After a bit it begins to work. It's wonderful the way it works. We tell each other things you never imagine you will. (*Pause.*) The reason I didn't leave my books at home is because once I came back and they were in the bath. Floating in the bath. My dad. Afterwards he's sorry.

Paula I think groups are crap. My presence here is tactical.

Emma enters. Flustered.

Emma I'm looking for Miranda.

Paula She's not here.

Emma She should be here.

Paula But she's not here.

Nicola She'll be here in a minute. Have you come for the group?

Emma Well, now I don't know what to do. I probably haven't brought a pen. (*She rummages in her bag.*)

Paula What are you in for?

Emma What? Oh. I'm not . . . I'm a friend of Miranda's. I'm not . . . shit. I'll leave her a note. (*She roots in her bag once more.*) No pen. Could you say that Emma came. She came and she had to go. Something came up. Thank you for suggesting I came in the first place. I'm all right. I just have to pull myself together. Love Emma. So. Emma.

13

Came. Went. Okay now. Sorry. Love etc. . . .

Miranda enters and Emma sits down quickly.

Shit.

Miranda Hello. Have you all met?

They nod. Miranda sits.

I'll just say a few words as it's our first meeting. Welcome.
I know it isn't easy joining a group and I want to say congratulations for getting here. For taking that first step. In
the past I've found that groups such as these can offer the
support and encouragement necessary to enable us to create positive change in our lives at stressful or difficult
times. I've kept it women only because, well, it speaks for
itself really. (*Pause.*) Women often find it easier to share in
an all-woman environment. (*Pause.*) Would anyone like to
start?

Pause. They sit in silence.

Nicola I'd just like to say that I'm very glad to be here.

Emma I don't think I should be here. I'm sorry, Miranda.
I was just feeling confused. I must be at a sort of turning
point in my life. But turning to what? Miranda . . . we're
friends . . . is it okay to tell them, Miranda? I'm not really
one of you. Miranda was telling me about the group and
then I just thought, God, I'm in such a mess. I have to do
something. This is my opportunity. This group. But now,
sitting here, I'm thinking what on earth was I thinking?

Miranda People often feel uncomfortable at the first
meeting.

Nicola I could start if you like?

Miranda That's very generous of you, Nicola. Nicola was
in a group I ran before.

Nicola My dad doesn't like me going out of the flat. I think he's scared of being on his own. I'm finding it quite hard to leave him on his own.

Miranda I think we should start with some role work. You be yourself, Nicola.

Nicola stands.

Emma, would you be Nicola's dad?

Nicola Geoff.

Emma Geoff?

Miranda Emma, you respond to Nicola as if you were Geoff.

Emma But what sort of person is he?

Miranda A person that doesn't like being alone.

Emma That could be anybody.

Paula A desperate fucker.

Miranda We used this technique before very successfully, didn't we, Nicola?

Nicola Yes.

Emma But what do I say?

Nicola Dad?

Emma Have we started?

Nicola Dad?

Emma Yes? I'm sorry I've forgotten your name.

Nicola Nicola. I'm going out now, Dad.

Emma Out?

Nicola Yes. Out.

Emma Out?

Nicola Yes.

Emma Okay, Nicola.

Nicola Don't get upset, Dad.

Emma I'm not getting upset.

Nicola Well, you usually do. You usually tell me not to go.

Emma Oh. Don't go.

Nicola I have to, Dad. I'm studying. My exams are next month.

Emma Well, all right then. Seeing as it's your education that's at stake.

They stop there. Nicola looks over to Miranda.

Miranda I think you got your permission to leave a little easily, Nicola. But you remained calm and logical, which was an effective strategy. Do you want to say anything?

Nicola I thought Emma did very well.

Emma I was awful.

Miranda Try swapping over.

Nicola You can have my bag. He sits in the chair facing the telly.

She gives her bag to Emma. Sits down, centre.

Miranda (*to Emma*) You're Nicola.

Emma Oh. I see. I'm Nicola. (*She prepares herself and begins.*) I'm going out now, Dad. I have my exams to do. I want to get on in life. So I'm going out now. Goodbye.

Nicola stares straight ahead.

I said goodbye. (*Pause.*) Aren't you going to say goodbye
back?

Nicola Drip drip drip.

Emma What?

Nicola There's a drip, Nick. Kitchen ceiling.

Emma I'll have a look when I get back.

Nicola Are you going to pass then?

Emma That's the idea.

Nicola Then off to college. Wizz bang. Corks pop. A
degree used to be a passport to something. To a job actually. That was in the old days when there were jobs.
Seriously though, Nick, a vocational degree is better than
some piss-farty thing. Psychology.

Emma Well, I have to be going.

Nicola Psych-ology. What am I going to do?

Emma You can watch the telly.

Nicola Five o'clock, Nick.

Emma Another hour and it'll get going.

Nicola Excessive use of hyperbole, Nick. Telly never gets
going. Telly is a stream of pale lumpless puke that consistently fails to become projectile.

Emma Oh, well. Read the paper.

Nicola Have you read it?

Emma No.

Nicola Too much time on my hands, that's my problem.
I've read it. What's your opinion on wine, Nick?

Emma It's a drink.

17

Nicola Education's not been wasted on you, has it? There's one whole page given over to the glory of wine. A picture too, just in case we don't know what a bottle looks like. Pinot Noir, Pouilly Fuise. I don't expect it means anything to you, does it? Could be dog's-piss wine, couldn't it? French – much too sensible a subject. No 'ology' in it.

Emma I don't drink wine.

Nicola You need money to drink it. Is that what you mean? And I could never afford it?

Emma No.

Nicola I'm thinking of the future. I worry about you, Nick. There you'll be one day, discussing psychology and drinking arse water. We are the hollow men. I've upset myself now. Skip your class. Just this once, Nick. I feel low.

Emma I can't.

Nicola It can't hurt, can it? Just to miss it once. I don't want to be on my own, Nick. Not tonight. I get these thoughts.

Emma Well, you could save them up and tell them to me later. When I get back. After I've been out.

Nicola Aren't you handling me well? Wouldn't your friend Miranda be pleased. You've contained my aggressive negativity. Skip it. This once. Won't hurt. For me. Please. Please, love. Please.

Emma seems stuck.

We could talk.

Emma is still stuck. Nicola comes to her rescue.

But you've made a commitment.

Emma Yes.

Nicola That's right. To yourself.

Emma Yes.

Nicola Bye, love.

Emma manages to leave.

Miranda Well done, Nicola and Emma.

Emma How incredible. I mean, it was actually quite difficult to get out of the door.

Miranda Yes, he was making it hard for you.

Nicola He does love me. He's not like that all the time.

Emma He just kept talking. It's hard to say what about.

Miranda But you kept hold of your initial desire to leave.

Nicola He doesn't really talk to anyone except me.

Emma That was very interesting.

Miranda He uses that. You have rights too.

Emma I knew I was right to come. It's great to be here. Inspiring. Like old times.

Miranda Is there anything you'd like to say, Paula?

Paula Do we get a tea break?

SCENE FIVE

Miranda at home. She is working. Roger comes in from the kitchen. He has a bottle of wine and glasses.

Roger You're not working?

Miranda Yes, Roger, I am. I'm behind. Terribly behind.

Roger But you've only been back a fortnight. Friday night. Shouldn't you be taking things easy? Slowly but surely.

Miranda There is no such animal in social work.

Roger They did say, didn't they, at work, that you should take it easy? I was there, remember. The afternoon you came home.

Miranda I'm absolutely fine.

Roger Yes, of course. Of course you are.

Miranda Working helps.

Roger I've got some wine. I thought we could have a toast. To the old Miranda. It's good to have her back.

Miranda I'll have one later, thanks.

Roger Right, right.

Miranda I really do just have to finish this. (*She continues to work.*)

Roger I suppose I could do some work. (*He doesn't move.*) Yes. I don't seem to get time for it nowadays. You know, four years ago no one in my department had even heard the word module. Now everything's modules, modules. The whole department has gone modular. It's like a disease. A module is like a pill, you hand it to your students with a glass of water and say, 'Here, swallow when you can afford it.' (*He pours himself a drink.*) I looked it up the other day. A set course forming a unit in an educational scheme. Little words. Scheme: a plan pursued secretly, insidiously for private ends. Yes, I thought. Yes. Where have all the big words gone? Enlightenment. Growth.

Miranda Roger.

Roger Sorry. Sorry. (*Pause.*) The thing is, I spend half my time administrating my modules. They come with twice their bodyweight in paper. Where am I supposed to get any time for my bloody Hegel?

Miranda It is harder now, Roger, but you'll make time.

Roger Yes, yes. You need a good text behind you in order to create the right sort of modular appeal.

Miranda (*still working*) You've got a text behind you.

Roger Fifteen years behind me. It doesn't count.

Miranda You could do some work now.

Roger ponders this. Sound of someone entering.

Roger That's Emma. I think the idea is we have a bit of a celebration.

Miranda I'm working.

He jumps up. Emma enters, carrying a bag of shopping.

Emma Happy second week back!

Miranda Thank you.

Emma I went along to Miranda's group, Roger. It was fantastic. I'm cooking. (*She indicates the bag.*) Shall we have a drink? Oh, Roger's started! Yes please, Roger.

Roger pours her a drink. Miranda puts her work to one side.

I'd just like to say a few things. About me. You've been brilliant, both of you. Such good friends. Letting me treat this like a second home, listening to me go on and on about Alan. It must have been really boring. Anyway, cheers.

Roger It wasn't boring. Was it, Miranda?

Miranda It's fantastic that you're on your feet again, Emma.

Emma Yes. In fact I just wanted to run something by you.

Roger Sure.

Emma The thing is, I don't want criticism. I feel that what I need at this point are warm agreeing eyes looking at me.

Roger Okay.

Miranda How can we approve of something before we've heard what it is?

Emma I knew you'd be critical.

Miranda Well, I could leave the room for five minutes and Roger can sit here nodding and smiling. How's that?

Emma That would be silly. It's your house. Well, just let me finish what I have to say before you interrupt. (*Pause.*) I met this woman. She has a business in occasion cards and she wants to expand and she's looking for a partner. Someone with a good eye. Artistic flair. I could put in some of the money that Alan gave me. New occasions are being invented all the time. Congratulations on your first holiday together card. Or, sorry to hear of the death of your pet.

Pause.

Miranda What about your painting?

Emma I knew you'd say that. I haven't done that for a while, Miranda. That's what I've been trying to tell you.

Miranda But you'll start again soon.

Emma I just don't seem to get round to it.

Miranda It's Alan's fault. He used you, Emma.

Emma Yes, I know.

Miranda Chopping his salads when you should have been doing your work.

Emma I know. I was stupid. But sometimes he couldn't get the staff.

Miranda He couldn't get them for free.

Emma Alan was paying the mortgage. I felt guilty.

Miranda Well, it's over now. You can get back to what you want to do.

Emma These cards.

Miranda You can't be serious about this, Emma. You're an artist. You don't want to get involved in some half-baked business venture that'll collapse in six months.

Emma She seemed a nice woman.

Pause.

Miranda Do you know where I drove past yesterday? Salt Street.

Roger Did you?

Miranda It's been converted into flats. We could never afford a house like that now. I stopped the car and looked. It always seemed such a sunny house.

Emma That's to do with the position of the windows.

Miranda And memories. Good memories.

Emma If Alan was here it could be like then – the four of us.

Miranda But Alan isn't here.

Emma No. Alan is officially a bastard. (*Pause.*) What I remember is talking. Lots of people talking and talking. You and Roger stayed up for nights discussing whether

23

his penis was an instrument of patriarchy.

Roger It rings a faint bell.

Miranda We found a *Playboy* in Alan's room and we ritually burnt it, didn't we, Emma?

Emma You'd read *The Female Eunuch*.

Miranda I remember feeling fantastic. Watching it burn.

Roger Arguably the most radical revolution of the twentieth century is the feminist one. Woman shaking off her chains.

Miranda And your painting is part of that, Emma.

Emma Roger's got a little paunch!

Roger Oh God, have I?

Emma Just then you looked like a faun, Roger. A saggy old faun.

Roger God, how alarming.

Emma Yes, we're all getting older.

Miranda What a revelation.

Roger The thing is, I'm not sure what position I take on jogging.

Emma What position?

Roger Politically. For me jogging has become the primary spectacle of the mass leisure market. The nexus of sport and capitalism.

Miranda Also you've lost one of your trainers.

Emma Alan goes jogging. He's very up on these things. He's in a men's group now, Roger.

Roger Jesus, is he?

Miranda That's no bad thing.

Roger I suppose not.

Miranda Men wanting to empower women.

Emma It's not that sort of group, Miranda. This is a nineties version. They go into the woods and beat drums. It helps them succeed in business. It's an American import. It's very primeval and that's why they're always jogging.

Roger Extraordinary.

Miranda Pathetic.

Emma With jogging you have to have a planned programme, Roger. London's full of poor old joggers dropping dead from sudden exertion.

Miranda Roger's not old, he's fifty-one.

Roger Fifty. Fifty!

Miranda Fifty-one.

Roger Jesus. Am I?

Emma Marlon Brando.

Roger That's incredible.

Emma He's fat but he still get's fucked.

Roger Somehow psychologically I'd lost a year.

Emma So you see you've no need to worry, Roger.

Miranda You're obssessed.

Emma Obssessed?

Miranda With bodies, age.

Emma It's all right for you. You've got Roger.

Miranda I haven't 'got' anybody.

Emma You're not trawling like I am.

Miranda Trawling?

Emma Picking over the scrawny left-behinds for life's partner. It's so degrading. I could kill Alan. He only had to stick around another twenty years and then he would have died. I don't want to be alone for the rest of my life.

Miranda You don't have to be alone.

Emma I'm forty-six. I have no significant other.

Miranda You have friends, Emma. You have your work.

Emma But who'll go on holiday with me? Who do I plan my retirement home with? I don't know if I can hold down another meal for one!

Miranda You're making yourself sound desperate.

Emma I'm sorry. That's how I feel. (*Pause.*) Are you where you expected to be, Miranda?

Miranda Approximately.

Emma Do you wish you'd ever had children?

Miranda No.

Emma Somehow you seem to be on track and I don't seem to be.

Miranda You're just healing. Getting over something.

Emma When Alan left I got down on my hands and knees and begged him to stay.

Miranda Oh.

Emma If you think about it, 'Oh' is just a hole.

Miranda It's an expression of mild concern.

Emma It's a hole. What do holes stand for? Graves or emptiness. Alan was my bung. The bung to stuff up my hole. My problem is I've lost my bung.

Roger I'm beginning to feel a twinge on Alan's behalf.

Emma I sleep with his coat. I try to be strong and worthy of your friendship but I just don't seem able to manage it.

Miranda Things will get better, Emma.

Emma What if they don't?

Miranda Well, I suppose that's up to you. You can decide you can't survive in the big wicked world without Alan. Or you can face things and be a human being. You've got us. We'll support you.

Emma You're right. Of course you're right. You've been very good to me. I'll start the food. (*She exits quickly.*)

Roger Do you want some help?

A smashing sound. Emma re-enters holding broken bowl.

Emma I'm sorry.

Miranda Don't worry.

Emma Oh. God, I'm so clumsy.

Miranda It's only a bowl. Don't worry.

Emma But it was your favourite. I must be feeling a bit shaky. I'm sorry.

Roger We'll be able to glue that.

Emma God, I'm useless sometimes. And I've forgotten the cream. I'll go round the corner.

Roger I'll go shall I?

Emma No, no. My mistake. (*She takes her coat, hurries out.*)

Miranda Might as well throw that away. (*Indicates bowl.*)

Roger Really?

Miranda It's a sort of aggression against me. I don't want to be reminded of it.

Roger Against you?

Miranda Lost people hate us because they need us.

Roger Is Emma lost?

Miranda What do you think?

Roger But Emma never used to be lost. How would someone know if they were lost?

Miranda You're not lost, Roger.

Roger Oh, I know that. I know that. I was just thinking,

Miranda My clients make our lives look like heaven.

Roger Sure, sure. We're steeped in privilege. (*Pause.*) Have a drink?

Miranda You have a drink. I must get on.

Roger I just thought we could have a drink together.

SCENE SIX

The intercom. We hear Emma's voice in the dark: 'Hello.' The buzz of the intercom. The Hooded Man lets Emma into his flat.

Emma Do you always wear that?

28

Hooded Man When I knew it was you. In your honour.

Emma You needn't have bothered. I'm bringing these back. (*She shows him the gloves.*)

Hooded Man Oh.

Emma I left with them last time. It was a mistake.

Hooded Man Thanks.

Emma I wasn't sure you'd be in. I was going to push them through the letter box. I'm actually a very honest person.

Hooded Man Yes. Thank you. Would you like a drink?

Emma No. I better go.

Hooded Man Well. Thanks. (*He holds up the gloves.*)

Emma You should have said something.

Hooded Man I should have. You're right.

Emma You shouldn't have just sprung it on me. Coming out of the bathroom like that.

Hooded Man I know. I apologize.

Emma It's not what you expect on a first date.

Hooded Man Sorry. To be honest, I thought it might be best to plunge you straight in.

Emma Plunge me?

Hooded Man Rubberists are experiencing a scarcity of female partners.

Emma You do surprise me.

Hooded Man But with you I took a gamble.

Emma Why?

Hooded Man I don't know. I was acting on instinct I suppose.

Emma Do you mean that you instinctively saw something in me?

Hooded Man Just an instinct.

Emma What did you see?

Hooded Man And then I knew when you took the gloves.

Emma Knew what?

Hooded Man I suppose it's a primitive thing. An exchange.

Emma I felt awkward, that's why I took them. I felt socially compromised.

Hooded Man Accepting something. It's a pun.

Emma Don't go all bloody literary on me.

Hooded Man You have a natural proclivity to anger. I like that.

Emma I'm not an angry person.

Hooded Man I think people get strait-jacketed into what's considered a normal sex life and then they never feel free to experiment. Then they have to be shocked into something new.

Emma Plunged.

Hooded Man Yes.

Emma How did you get into all this rubber?

Hooded Man With a wellington boot. As a child I was repeatedly struck on the buttocks with a wellington boot.

Emma Really?

Hooded Man No. Not at all. I just like rubber. It's slippery, smooth and it twangs.

Emma I think you must have some sort of dreadful problem.

Hooded Man I just like to unwind in my free time.

Emma Why don't you play golf like other people?

Hooded Man You were getting into it.

Emma I was not.

Hooded Man It seemed to me that you were getting into it.

Emma It's just silly. Inside I was laughing at how stupid you looked.

Hooded Man There was a connection between us in the eyes.

Emma I was thinking, God, this is one for the diary.

Hooded Man It's not the sort of game you can play on your own. That's how I know. From when you took the gloves.

Emma Bollocks to the gloves. You see, this is all so typically male. Violence is sexy. And there's no feelings. Nothing between us. It's all to do with patriarchy. I even bother to return your poxy property. A typical caring woman. Really I should burn the f-ing things.

Hooded Man You are a goddess.

Emma My name is Emma.

Hooded Man Please burn them. They cost twenty four pounds.

Emma You evil little worm.

Hooded Man gets to his knees.

Hooded Man I'm wriggling at your feet.

Emma You ought to be careful. I could be insane. I must be when you stop to think about it. I could put my foot on your neck and crush it and crush it till it snapped.

Hooded Man Put your foot on my neck.

Emma You really are asking for trouble.

Hooded Man I know.

Emma I could do it.

Hooded Man I know.

Emma I could. (*Pause.*) Oh God. Oh my God.

Hooded Man What?

Emma Something terrible has happened.

Hooded Man What?

Emma I want to press harder.

Hooded Man Press harder.

Emma I want to press harder.

Hooded Man We can swap over later. I've got a spare hood in the bedroom.

He exits, she follows.

SCENE SEVEN

Paula in Miranda's office. 7 p.m. She has Victoria on her lap. Victoria is eating a packet of crisps.

Paula Don't tell me. I know. I know. I did a stupid thing.

I couldn't help myself. We just got on the train, didn't we, Victoria?

Victoria eats, nods.

We had a brilliant day. We went to *Baywatch the Movie*. Then we went to Burger King. I said to Victoria, do you want to go back to the Clements or do you want to come home with me, and she said, I want to come home with you, Mum, didn't you?

Victoria We had king-size chips.

Miranda I'll phone the Clements now. (*She picks up phone, dials.*)

Paula I know it looks bad.

Victoria When that man was drowning, right, how come he wasn't eaten by a shark?

Paula Because it wasn't a film with a shark in. Sharks cost money. It was cheap film.

Miranda Hello. Hello. It's Miranda Hurst. Yes. Yes. She's here with me now.

Paula Don't stuff all those in at once, Victoria. It's not nice.

Victoria I'm chewing them.

Paula You're swallowing them whole.

Miranda Well, if that's convenient for you

Victoria chews open-mouthed to demonstrate.

Victoria We're doing Africa at school, Mum.

Paula Yeah.

Miranda Yes, of course.

Victoria Africa's a continent not a country.

Paula Shhh. No one said it was a country.

Miranda That would be fine.

Victoria It's a very common mistake to make.

Paula What's that on your T-shirt?

Victoria It's called Eurocentrism.

Paula It's called ice-cream.

Miranda Thank you so much.

She tickles Victoria, who laughs.

Mr Clements will meet you at the station. That's very kind of him. I think Victoria is old enough for me to speak frankly to you both. In the long run this sort of thing doesn't help you to be together. It's just painful for everybody.

Paula I'm only fucking human. Don't you use words like that, Victoria.

Victoria Words like human?

Miranda You're going back to the Clements' house, Victoria. Do you understand why?

Victoria I don't want to go back. They eat funny.

Paula She doesn't want to go back. What you don't understand is that you can't keep taking things away from people, it fucks up their heads.

Miranda Would you wait outside for a minute, Victoria. There's a chair by the door.

Paula Go on, love. Take your comic.

Victoria This is my new T-shirt, Pocahontas. (*She exits.*)

Miranda What happened?

Paula It just seemed right at the time. We had a nice day. Then you think, why has it got to end? Who says?

Miranda I do understand. It is hard. But it's no solution, is it? Running back to London with her. (*Pause.*) I would like your asurance that it won't happen again.

Paula It won't happen again.

Miranda When I discuss your case with the team, I'll emphasize that this was an isolated incident.

Paula Thanks. (*She lights a cigarette.*)

Miranda There is another thing.

Paula Not the pissing group again?

Miranda No.

Paula I haven't sorted out my GCSEs if that's what you mean.

Miranda No, it's about money.

Paula Oh, yes, I've got your money. Thanks.

She gives Miranda twenty quid.

Miranda What I was wondering was where you got the money? For the cinema, Victoria's train fare, the T-shirt?

Paula What do you mean?

Miranda I was wondering where you got the money?

Paula What?

Miranda The money. I really can't overlook it. I'm asking.

Paula I couldn't go down there with no money, Miranda.

Pause.

I'm not ashamed. I took ten minutes out of my life and I gave a man a blow job.

Miranda I'm not judging you. I understand that women get desperate and as a last resort . . .

Paula That's your O-level prostitution talking.

Miranda It's a serious matter.

Paula It's nothing. It's easy. I start off with my hand. I only put it in my mouth for the last bit. When it's hard.

Miranda I don't want the details.

Paula I thought that would be one of the perks.

Miranda On the contrary.

Paula It's a sort of social work in a way. I provide the service their wives can't handle.

Miranda Do you take these clients home?

Paula What?

Miranda Do you take them home?

Paula No. I do not.

Miranda I don't know if I believe that, Paula.

Paula I wouldn't take them home if Victoria was there, would I?

Miranda You are a bright, capable person, Paula, and you have to start believing in the future. In yourself.

Paula Or what?

Miranda It's up to you. I can only support you if you want my support. Or you jeopardize everything. You'll need to explain to Victoria about going back. I'll see you at the group, Paula.

Pause. Paula opens the door.

Paula Victoria.

Victoria comes in.

You go back to the Clements. It's not for ever. Just till Mum gets back on her feet. It won't be long.

Victoria How long, Mum?

Paula Not long I said, didn't I? Now, get your jacket on.

Victoria puts her jacket on.

Victoria How long, Mum?

Miranda takes them to the door. They exit.

SCENE EIGHT

Roger sits alone. He does not work. Emma enters Miranda and Roger's front room.

Emma It's me.

Roger Miranda's working late.

Emma walks about restlessly.

Do you want to take off your coat?

Emma Oh my God, I've done something terrible.

Roger I'm sure it was nothing too terrible.

Emma I feel awful. It's hard having Miranda as a friend. It's hard to live up to.

Roger I know. I know. Don't worry.

Emma I do worry, Roger, I do. You don't know what I

am. Miranda doesn't know. If she knew I don't think she'd like me.

Roger I think you're being very hard on yourself. I'm sure you haven't done anything much.

Emma How would you know?

Roger Well, I don't actually know. But I do know you, so I was happy to conclude that I was sure that you hadn't done anything much.

Emma Bollocks.

Roger Would you like a drink, Emma?

Emma What I hate is sure people. People who are always so bloody sure. (*She takes off her top.*)

Roger What are you doing?

Emma I'm surprising you. I'm showing you that you don't know anybody. You don't know what they've done and you couldn't begin to guess.

Roger Please put on your jumper.

Emma No. I'm going to sit here in my bra and have a fag and give myself cancer. Any objections? Because you're a decent and good person, Roger, you think everyone else is decent and good too. But we're not. Some of us are murky.

Roger Emma.

Emma No. I've done something. Something sickening and if you try to calm me down I'll scream. You'd never understand, Roger.

Roger I might.

Emma No, you're too . . .

Roger Too . . . ?

Emma Flattened. Sorry.

Roger Flattened?

Emma Don't take it the wrong way.

Roger Flattened?

Emma It's not a bad thing to be. It's safe at least.

  Pause.

Roger I did something.

Emma What? You did?

Roger Yes. I don't know how it happened. She's a student. She's twenty years old. She's French, from the border with Belgium, actually. She's in my Hegelian thought module. Anyway, I found her attractive. It was the end of term and I'd had a bottle of wine. It was the end of term party and we . . . and we . . .

Emma Try to breathe and talk at the same time, Roger.

Roger The terrible thing is it was when Miranda was sick. That's the thing. When she was sick. How wretched.

Emma Have you done anything since?

Roger No, no. I haven't. I swear I haven't.

Emma Oh well, forget it.

Roger Forget it?

Emma It's nothing really. Christ, on Thursday I went home with a strange man who tied me up, wore a hood and called me obscene names while I spat at his navel.

Roger Really?

Emma Safe sex.

They look at each other.

Roger We crept into the gardens. It was dark. When I felt her skin it was a shock. Such young skin and mine seemed old. I seemed on the edge of being irretrievably old. And I reached out and held on. A pang. Unbearably fantastic.

Emma Well, now we're partners in crime. Have a cigarette.

She offers him one, he hesitates.

Don't worry. If you catch alight I'm good in an emergency.

He moves towards her.

No kissing.

SCENE NINE

The group.

Miranda Do you want to talk about what happened to you last week, Paula?

Paula I kidnapped my own kid. It lasted two hours. I was bollocked. The end. By Paula.

Miranda It must have been difficult leaving her.

Paula Yes, it was. Victoria wet herself on the train home.

Miranda That must have been upsetting. Do you want to explore that with the group?

Nicola I could be Victoria if you like.

Paula No you can't. You're nothing like Victoria. She's sensible and charismatic.

Miranda I think what we're saying is that there's a space

40

for you to do that, Paula, if you want it.

Paula No thank you.

Miranda arranges two chairs as an interview room.

Miranda Something different. Nicola, you're interviewing Paula for job. Paula's got an interview coming up. For a cashier.

Paula I won't get it.

They begin.

Nicola Do sit down.

Paula sits.

Nicola Now, Paula.

Paula Yes.

Nicola Can you tell me a little about your past work experience?

Paula I haven't got any. Do you mind if I smoke?

Nicola We do have a no-smoking policy in this building.

Paula Smoking helps me think.

Nicola We do have a lot of applications for this post.

Paula Yes, but that's not because it's a good job. It's because people can't afford to be choosy. It's not something you'd lie in bed dreaming about.

Nicola Our staff tell us they're quite happy. We have a very good staff–management relationship.

Paula But you don't know what they say behind your back.

Nicola What do they say behind our back?

Paula I'm not going tell you, am I? It might prejudice my chances.

Miranda Do you want this job, Paula?

Paula Yes.

Miranda Well, just try to keep focused on that. How did it go from your point of view, Nicola?

Nicola Well, not too good.

Miranda Would you have given her the job?

Pause.

Nicola Probably not. Depends if we were desperate.

Paula Desperate?

Miranda Try swapping over.

Nicola 'knocks' on the door.

Paula Just a minute. (*to Miranda*) That's what they do. To make you feel more nervous. Come in. Yes, you must be Ranjit.

Nicola No, Paula.

Paula Oh, yes, of course. I don't expect you've got qualifications or you wouldn't be here. Now, why do you want to come and work for us?

Nicola Well, it's about my life.

Paula What about your life?

Nicola I want another chance. There's certain things I want to be able to do in my life and getting a job is all part of that. I really want a job. Then I can break all my old patterns. I can start to restructure my life. I'll go to work in the morning. I'll probably make a few friends at work. New people. So I won't be miserable going. I'll look forward to seeing them. And maybe some of the customers. We might have chats sometimes. And at the end of the day I will be tired but it won't be the sort of tired when you're sitting around all day watching bad TV and smoking. It will feel like a positive tiredness. And then I'll go and pick up my little girl from school. And then I'll cook her tea and we'll talk. We'll talk about our day. I'll say the things that happened to me and she'll say the things that happened to her. Sometimes I might have to help her with something. A problem that's cropped up. And that will make me feel glad because I'll have been able to help. I'll have been able to do something to help someone I really love.

Paula That was brilliant!

Miranda Nicola. Well done.

Paula Fucking excellent.

Nicola sits down.

Still, if you said that in real life they'd think you were off your case.

Miranda I think they'd sympathize with the spirit of it. What do you think, Emma? Would you give her the job?

Emma What? Oh. Yes. I suppose so.

Miranda Is there something you'd like to talk to us about?

Emma Yes. Wish me luck. I'm going into the occasion-card business.

Miranda So you're giving up on the painting?

Emma Yes. After decades of being ignored by the art world I've finally taken the hint.

Miranda Emma is a wonderful painter. She did a portrait

43

of us together once. She called it sisters.

Nicola That's fantastic. There must have been a real feeling of sisterhood then. Back then.

Emma Oh, yes. It was sisterhood this and sisterhood that.

Paula I don't talk to my sister. She's a cow.

Miranda Well, there are often complicated dynamics that arise between siblings.

Paula She's a fucking cow. There's something evil inside her that's always been there. She wouldn't have Victoria when I went away. That's why I'm in this mess.

Emma That's what's so terrifying. What's inside you that you never knew about. Our next-door neighbours had a tortoise. Something about the size of a shoe used to set it off. They'd all be sitting there on a Sunday with their G and Ts, all chatting and laughing and then one of them would look down and scream because Finbar was shagging their plimsole. There'd be a cry and a clattering sound as he was booted off and bounced across the York stone.

Nicola That doesn't sound normal to me. Maybe they disturbed his hibernation patterns.

Emma He was obeying something primitive.

Miranda His deep attraction to footwear. What are we really talking about here, Emma?

Emma Pets. Something was driving that tortoise.

Paula He was a randy little bugger.

Emma A natural force.

Nicola Tortoises have bad eyes. It was probably all a mistake.

Emma I mean, what's disgusting and what isn't and who decides?

Nicola Anything that hurts someone is disgusting.

Paula Anything that takes longer than five minutes to clear up.

Miranda I think people know that nothing done with love is disgusting.

Paula So if Finbar loved that plimsole he's okay. If he just fancied it he's a pervert.

Emma You see, people can get strait-jacketed into what's considered a normal sex life and they never feel free to experiment.

Miranda Are you worried because you're sleeping with Alan's coat?

Emma What?

Paula Whose coat?

Miranda It hardly qualifies you for inclusion in the category of sexual peversion.

Emma You didn't have to mention the coat. Now everyone knows I'm a weak and stupid person who sleeps with a man's coat because that's all she can manage.

Miranda Nobody thinks that, Emma.

Emma That's the thing with these groups. You come along with all these expectations and somehow they make you feel worse. Smaller.

Miranda Is that really your experience of them, Emma?

Emma Once I was in a consciousness-raising group and we passed a waste-paper bin round and we all tipped our make-up into it.

Paula What for?

Emma Make-up was oppressive.

Paula But it makes you look a fuck of a lot better.

Nicola (*to Emma*) I think that's brilliant.

Emma That's because I haven't finished. Later I sneaked back and got my mascara.

Paula Good for you.

Nicola Why?

Emma I have small eyes.

Miranda You have perfectly fine eyes.

Emma You have perfectly fine eyes. I have small eyes. I was supposed to pretend I had perfectly fine eyes and that I felt fine but what I really felt was ugly and stupid for minding about it. But that was the last thing you were ever allowed to admit to. It was all like that. Lots of pretending.

Miranda I had no idea you felt like that. I never did.

Emma It was like a sort of conspiracy. You were shut out if you said anything wrong.

Paula Women are bitchy.

Nicola There's an excellent book you should read: *Man Made Language*.

Paula You know how to enjoy yourself, Nick.

Miranda Emma. This is unbelievable.

Emma No it isn't. I'm still afraid to say things.

Miranda There's nothing you can't talk about here. If you want to sell birthday cards you should discuss it here.

Really face what you're leaving behind.

Emma All right. In the past I wanted to be an artist. A very good woman artist. I felt I had a mission. Because behind us were centuries of women who had been denied the opportunity to express themselves. Whose talent had been stamped out.

Nicola And what happened?

Emma Time sort of went on. I had a few small exhibitions. One in Brighton, one in a small gallery in North London under some railway arches. I used to paint in a little room at the top of the house and it became harder and harder to climb the stairs. I drank at lunchtimes and napped in the afternoon. I did a bit of teaching. Then this thing called conceptual art happened. There were exhibits entitled 'Condom Hardening under Glass'. I was lost, I suppose. What it took me a while to understand was that I didn't have any talent.

Nicola Yes, yes, you did. I'm sure you did.

Emma No. You have to have the sort of passion a mother has for a child. I never felt that. I was just average. So you see, I was sort of fooled.

Miranda We were a bit naive. Your work was resisted because it challenged the status quo.

Nicola That must be it.

Emma I had an idea of myself that was nothing like who I was.

Miranda I loved your paintings. Your painting, Emma. That one of us. Take it to a gallery.

Emma I can't. They won't be interested.

Miranda Take it to a gallery run by a woman.

Emma That's no guarantee of anything.

Miranda Try.

Emma There's nothing I'd like more than to be good. But I'm not good enough, I'm not. And it's taken a lot to get to this point.

Nicola Why are you arguing?

Emma Maybe everything was a big fucking mistake. Have you ever thought of that, Miranda?

Nicola Why are you shouting at Miranda?

Miranda It wasn't a mistake. It's all right, Nicola.

Emma Just do this and this and all the good talented things inside you will come out. Abandon the life of your mothers. Well, I did and now I've got nothing. No career, no husband, no child. Nothing's turned out the way it was supposed to.

Pause.

Miranda Perhaps things haven't turned out the way we wanted. Maybe the world we imagined was so miraculous that it's not possible that it could exist. I remember waking up one morning. There were a group of us squatting a building we wanted for a women's refuge. It was freezing. I could hear birds and this feeling shot through me. At first I didn't know what it was and then I realized it was joy. Just joy. I thought, I am where I want to be. I am doing totally what I want to do and believe I should be doing and it is completely liberating. No energy wasted in doubt or despair. A moment of absolute certainty. You choose to go on acting on that faith because you know it's the best thing you've got.

Emma I can't come any more. Don't try to make me stay.

Before Emma can leave Nicola begins.

Nicola Dad? Dad? Are you asleep?

(*as Geoff*) I wasn't asleep.

Nicola You shouldn't have waited up for me, Dad, if you're tired.

(*as Geoff*) I was thinking about Greece. It's a beautiful country, Nicola. Full of decayed classicism. The islands are especially beautiful, white chalky houses and a deep blue sea.

Nicola Sounds beautiful.

(*as Geoff*) I said that, Nicola. You're supposed to think of a conversation opener now, Nicola, like 'When was the last time you visited Greece?'or 'How long does the boat take from Athens to the islands?'

Nicola I think I'll go to bed now, Dad.

(*as Geoff*) I went to Greece with your mum, Nick. We were a bit hippyish. I've got the photo. I looked funny, didn't I? Sandals, beard, flappy-bottomed trousers.

Nicola I want to do a bit of reading before I crash out. Exams in a month.

(*as Geoff*) Do you think of her much, Nick?

Nicola Yes.

(*as Geoff*) Your poor mum. Poor Deirdre. We thought it was just tiredness. It was when the nausea started that a bell rang for me. A bell, low, threatening thunder.

Nicola Dad.

(*as Geoff*) Terrible pain.

Nicola Dad.

(*as Geoff*) Bottomless.

Nicola Dad.

(*as Geoff*) She was in pain at the end. Couldn't swallow. Had to spit into a bowl. A tree grew out of her tongue. Very rare.

Nicola Dad. Stop it.

(*as Geoff*) Cancer. Drank myself to oblivion. Yum, yum.

Nicola Feel sick.

(*as Geoff*) A cold coming we had of it. Just the worst time of year for a journey and such a long journey.

Nicola gags. Bends over.

Miranda Nicola? It's all right. I'm here. I'm here. You're okay.

Miranda puts her arm round Nicola. Sits down with her. Paula lights a cigarette. Emma stands watching.

Paula I never meant what I said. About you being Victoria.

Emma Poor Nicola.

Miranda You're okay. You're okay.

Paula I've been to Greece. 1987. With Victoria's dad before he went back to his wife. We went to Mykonos. Fantastic. All night dancing. The men are very good-looking. We had beer for breakfast. We used to have it looking at the sea. The sound of the sea is very soothing. Just listening to the sea. That's because that's what a baby hears inside its mother. It hears a sound like the sound of the sea. A shush shush sound. But really it's the blood going in and out of the mother's heart. It's comforting. That's why we like the sound of the sea, apparently.

Miranda There's a story that the earth gave birth to the sea. That the earth was the most powerful goddess and the sea came from her belly.

Nicola I like that story.

Emma sits with group.

Act Two

SCENE ONE

Roger is standing by the phone. He hears Miranda come downstairs. He hurriedly sits down. Miranda enters.

Roger Emma was here.

Miranda What did she want?

Roger She wanted to see you. We talked about Alan mostly.

Miranda Emma. She's always managed to pick rotten men.

Roger Has she? Alan's not that bad, is he?

Miranda He had a thin veneer of PC. Underneath he was a latent Chef of the Year.

Roger He's opening a new restaurant apparently. Alan always seemed to be drifting. We used to think he was a bit of a joke. Now he must be gloating.

Miranda Would you be gloating if you were Alan? Alan isn't writing a book on Hegel.

Roger No.

Miranda You're making a lasting contribution, Roger. Alan is making crêpes.

Roger The thing is, I'd be gloating if I was Alan. I'd be thinking, 'Poor old Roger. His yeast isn't rising. He's got a paunch and a writing block and I've got two restaurants

52

and I'm minting it in.'

Miranda He's making money, Roger. What's that? It's just money. We've got much more than he's got. We're committed to living our lives with some sort of vision.

Roger In the morning I have leg cramps. What do you think that is?

Miranda I don't know. Are you feeling all right?

Roger I've just been sitting here drinking too much wine. Feeling sorry for myself. (*Pause.*) Why am I writing a book on Hegel?

Miranda You must know that.

Roger Because he said, 'History is the progress of reason in the world.' The other day it just slipped my mind. I sat there for three solid hours. I only wrote two sentences.

Miranda Maybe they were key sentences.

Roger Then I scribbled them out again.

Miranda Well things fell apart a bit when I was sick but I'm here now. (*Pause.*) All this stuff about Alan, I don't know where it's come from. And your book. You've been planning that for years. I was thinking. You were so sweet to me when I was ill. Force-feeding me vitamin Cs.

Roger Without vitamin C the body can't process any other vitamins.

Miranda I think we should plan a holiday. What was the name of that place we went to in France?

Roger Miranda? (*Pause.*) In fact it's funny that we've been talking about Alan because actually I've just been speaking to him on the phone.

Miranda Did he phone you?

Roger Well, one of us phoned one of us. For a chat. You know. Anyway, he asked me to come along to his group.

Miranda What group's that?

Roger His group. His men's group.

Miranda Oh.

Roger Yes. Yes. That's what I thought.

Miranda What did you think?

Roger Well, I thought 'oh' like you. Anyway I said I'd go. But I probably won't. The thing is, I have to make up my mind in the next five minutes. It's a weekend retreat. I've packed a bag. (*He pulls a bag out from behind a chair.*) But it doesn't mean I'm definitely going.

Miranda I thought you wanted to see a film tomorrow.

Roger Well, I did. I do. I did. Alan said some weird things.

Miranda What things?

Roger Men mustn't be afraid of being men.

Miranda What did he mean?

Roger I don't know. Ha ha. It's really a suspect and ridiculous statement with absolutely no attempt at historical contextualizing. Ha ha.

Miranda Very Alan.

Roger Yes, yes, precisely. Very Alan. I have to bring some tough boots, an outdoor winter jacket and my favourite poem.

Miranda What's that?

Roger 'The Jabberwocky'. Funnily enough that was Alan's choice when he was initiated.

Miranda Are you being initiated?

Roger No, no, no. I'm not even necessarily going.

Miranda It seems like you are.

Roger Am I? I just think I need a break. To get out of London. Clear my head. There are so many things going on in my head.

Miranda You could have talked to me about them.

Roger I know, I know. The thing is, I said I'd go.

Miranda I can tell you now what you'll think of it.

Roger A lot of silly, hung-up men. I thought I could look at it as a sociological experience. I've taken the tin opener. We drive down to Bournemouth tonight. Our hotel overlooks the seafront. We get non-seasonal rates. The idea is we get to see the dawn.

Miranda Well, happy dawn.

Roger Right. Right. (*He picks up his bag.*) What am I doing? I don't deserve you. I don't even want to go. I just said I would to Alan. On the spur of the moment.

Miranda Go on.

Roger Bye. You do understand. I'd rather be here with you.

He exits. Miranda stands uncertainly.

SCENE TWO

Paula, alone, outside, a phone box.

Paula Hello? Hello? Miranda? It's me. Paula. A phone box on the Old Kent Road. It's a sort of tramp's toilet.

I'm standing in fossilized tramp's pee. If I pass out half-way through you'll know why. I've just popped out from work. I don't want them listening. It's all right. So. Now I'm a taxpayer can I have my kid back? What? Sorry, a lorry. It's pissing down. It's like being in a sort of human car wash. So what did the team say? I know, I know. I can't wait until tomorrow. What's the decision? I wasn't expecting anything. Fuck those fucking lorries. Yes, yes. I heard. I heard. Why? I am settled into a routine. I've done a week. Yeah. Yeah. Stick to the plan. Another month. I know it's a process. What? Yeah, yeah. I'm okay. Me money's run out.

She puts down the phone. Stands. Exits. Sound of rain.

SCENE THREE

Greenwich park. A hilltop. Remnants of a small picnic. Paula looks tired. Nicola lies a short distance away, reading a textbook.

Victoria Mum?

Paula What?

Victoria Say 'fuzzy duck' very fast.

Paula No.

Victoria Why not?

Paula You know why not.

Victoria Mum?

Paula What?

Victoria What's an airwave?

Paula Does it matter? I'm having a rest. (*Pause.*) Here.

Have a doughnut.

Victoria What sort?

Paula How many sorts are there? If you want one have one. If not . . .

Victoria Are they from work again?

Paula Yes.

Victoria Grungenuts. Is Nicola a grunge? I'm going to ask her.

Paula Don't ask her.

Victoria What does your shop sell?

Paula Eveything all the time and it expects me to be there.

Victoria Does it sell buildings?

Paula Don't be stupid.

Victoria You said everything.

Paula There's no need to be stupid.

Victoria Patrick and Isobel don't say stupid.

Paula What do they say then?

Victoria Hasn't thoroughly comprehended.

Paula That means stupid.

Victoria It doesn't.

Paula It means stupid. Stupid. (*Pause.*) I didn't mean that. I've been really looking forward to today. To have you come down for the day. It's my day off. I get Wednesdays off.

Victoria Why?

Paula Instead of Sundays.

Victoria Patrick doesn't work on Sundays. Or Saturdays.

Paula Well, banks don't open then, do they?

Victoria No. We're going on holiday.

Paula What?

Victoria To Lyon.

Paula Where?

Victoria Isobel is half French.

Paula Fucking hell.

Victoria *Je m'appelle Victoria. Et je habite à Sussex.*

Paula All right. All right.

Victoria They're going to ask you if it's okay.

Paula Have a doughnut.

Victoria *Non merci.*

Paula Do you want a doughnut, Nick?

Nicola Oh, no thanks.

Paula Don't then. No one have one. (*She picks up the doughnuts and empties the bag.*) They are obviously crap.

Nicola They looked like really nice ones to me.

Victoria She's in a bad mood.

Nicola I'm sure she's not. Not today.

Victoria It's because of Lyon.

Nicola Is that a friend from school?

Victoria No, it's the third largest city in France.

Nicola Oh.

Victoria You don't want me to go.

Paula Go where you like. I can't stop you. You go to Lyon and don't worry about me slogging me guts out in some poxy job.

Victoria It's not my fault it's a poxy job.

Nicola It's not a bad job. It's a positive step. Isn't it, Paula?

Paula Yeah, all right, Nicola. Go for a run, Victoria.

Victoria Why?

Paula You've got too much energy.

Victoria Running's boring.

Paula Run to that tree and back, go on.

Victoria No. You do it.

Paula I'm warning you.

Victoria I want to go to Lyon.

Paula Shut up about Lyon.

Victoria I hate you.

Paula Don't say that you little cow.

> *Nicola begins to pick up the doughnuts and put them back in the bag*

Nicola Guess what. This morning Dad boarded up the windows. He wanted to make the windows safe. So he took all these bits of wood from crates and things and hammered them over the windows. Bang, bang.

Victoria What for?

Nicola He said there was a storm coming. The sort Noah had in the Bible.

Paula Remind him he lives in Peckham.

Nicola Yes.

Victoria He sounds like a loony.

Paula Victoria.

Victoria That's what you said.

Paula I did not.

Nicola Don't worry. Lunatic is a bit of an old-fashioned word. Now we tend to use the term mentally ill or mentally unstable. Everyone gets a bit fed up with their job sometimes, Victoria. It's natural. (*to Paula*) Thanks for letting me come. I needed to get out.

Paula You wouldn't do it, would you?

Nicola What?

Paula My job.

Nicola Well, I wouldn't want to do it for ever.

Paula Well, how long would you do it for?

Nicola For as long as I needed to. I mean it would be part of a plan. A longer-term plan. You have to think of where you'll be in five years or so. That's what Miranda says.

Paula So where will I be in five years?

Nicola I don't know. Where do you envisage you'll be?

Paula I envisage myself as older and smoking more fags.

Nicola What about good things?

Paula What about them?

60

Nicola Yes, what about them?

Paula God, this is a fucking depressing conversation.

Nicola It only seems depressing at the start but if we carried on things would seem better.

Paula What I hate is waking up every morning in temporary accommodation with no teabags. I'm twenty-nine, I want to feel good when I wake up. You make a plan, you think, 'Great, I'll stick to that.' Only it's too dull or it's too hard. No one's giving anything to me. The third largest city in France. I didn't fucking know that, did you? The thing is, Nick, I know I should want her to go. You know, love it that she gets the opportunity. That's how I should feel, but I don't.

Nicola One visit to France is worth months in the classroom. For learning the language.

Victoria Mum. Where will I go if they go on holiday? Will I be on my own?

Paula Come here. Give me a hug.

Victoria gives her a hug.

Tighter. Tighter.

Victoria hugs her tighter.

Till it hurts. You go on holiday, that's fine by me. Just fine. (*Pause.*) I've got friends of my own remember.

Victoria Who?

Paula Friends.

Victoria Michael? (*Pause.*) You went to prison.

Paula Ten out of ten, Victoria.

Victoria Mum.

Paula Yes?

Victoria I've done something.

Paula What?

Victoria I've wet myself.

Paula You haven't?

Nicola Oh dear, never mind. I've got a tissue.

She begins to wipe Victoria's legs.

Victoria Wart wart schlobb tomato. That's how lunatics speak. Amble scramble bum beehive doughnut burp.

SCENE FOUR

Roger at home. He has just come in from a jog and is still in his jogging clothes. Emma enters. She has been drinking.

Emma I've come to give Miranda this. (*She holds her painting wrapped in a blanket.*)

Roger Right.

Emma So how are you?

Roger Fine, fine. Splendid.

Emma You don't look splendid, you look puffy. Still fucking that French girl?

Roger Is that the painting Miranda mentioned?

Emma Don't you love Miranda?

Roger Yes.

Emma Then why are you doing it?

Roger I'm not doing it.

Emma Yes you are. You're making love with a twenty-year-old from the border with Belgium.

Roger It's something I intend putting an end to in the near future.

Emma Really?

Roger Yes, at present it's not something I'm quite in control of. It's like Shakespeare said, a sort of madness, or as the romantics would have it, a fever.

Emma Thank you, professor. Do you know what I think? (*She swigs from her bottle.*) I think you're like a boil that's popped. There's all this stuff in you and for years you've pretended to be as antiseptic as hell and now in late middle-age it's pushed its way to the surface and burst all over your life.

Roger Charming.

Emma I think you're despicable.

Roger I'm the first to admit I've behaved badly.

Emma Pus-y, disgusting.

Roger I took advantage of Miranda's sickness.

Emma What would Hegel say?

Roger He'd be very disappointed.

Emma I've a good mind to write him a letter. Put a spoke up his zeitgeist.

Roger Have we got a safe word?

Emma How about punt?

Roger Punt?

Emma Any objections?

Roger The means of transport or the currency?

Emma Take your pick. It's a free country. (*She takes out some rope and begins to tie Roger up.*)

Roger The means of transport.

Emma continues to tie Roger.

Emma It's not the sort of thing she's interested in.

Roger Who?

Emma The woman at the gallery, Roger. What's the matter, aren't you bloody listening?

Roger Yes, I'm your slave.

Emma I took my courage in both hands and asked her if she'd like to see my other work.

Roger And?

Emma Nope.

Roger I see. Oh dear.

Emma Oh deary, deary, dear. She's interested in African artefacts and postmodern installations.

Roger You can try somewhere else. You are the mistress of figurative representation.

Emma That's what sickens me about you people. Your horrible cheery optimism. You bob along in a sort of sickly dream world.

Roger We've only got an hour.

Emma It's a lovely painting. Miranda and me. We look all shiny. And there's some lilies.

Roger An hour might be pushing it.

Emma When I got up this morning I felt hopeful. I am such a dupe.

Roger That was one gallery, Emma. There must be thousands. Perhaps this isn't a good time.

Emma For what?

Roger To do this. Um . . . this.

Emma Why can't you say it?

Roger I don't know. It's not coming out.

Emma S and M, Roger. You people can't even say it.

Roger Why do you keep saying that? 'You people' like that.

Emma Because I'm referring to yourself and Miranda. You people. The boil people. (*She goes over to Roger, ruffles his hair. Unzips his jogging top. Sits down opposite him with her bottle.*) The title of this work is boiling point.

Roger Emma?

  No reply.

What are you doing?

Emma I'm just sitting here.

Roger Aren't you going to . . .?

Emma What?

Roger Start. What are you going to do to me, Emma?

Emma Don't get your hopes up, Roger. I'm going to wait till Mummy gets here and then I'm going to let her deal with it.

Roger Very good. Very good.

Emma What?

Roger This is a twist in the game. It's a twist in the game. (*Pause.*) You're not really going to let Miranda walk in on this? What is the point of that?

Emma Communication. You're a sort of living picture. I want Miranda to see the bollocks.

Roger This is about the painting. You're angry and upset because your painting was rejected and you feel hurt. Now you want to hurt someone in return. (*Pause.*) Miranda is working very hard at the moment. Too hard. But if you feel you want to destroy her, go ahead.

Emma You're destroying her too. Fucking about.

Roger But I'm going to stop. Miranda means more to me than anything else in the world. What's happening between us, Emma, is a sort of aberration. It's not us. Not who we are. It's a sort of hiccup.

Emma You always put such a happy sheen on things. But aren't we an ugly pair doing an ugly thing?

Roger Emma. I think you may be a little disturbed today. Today may not be a good day to do anything rash.

Emma has another drink.

Untie me please, Emma.

Emma Give me an explanation and I'll untie you. Make us all nice again and I'll be nice.

Roger We are nice. We are.

Emma Prove it to me. Oh, and listen. There's Mummy's car. I can hear the brakes go squealy squealy. Mummy needs some brake oil.

Roger Punt, Emma.

Emma Punt yourself.

Roger Punt, punt, punt.

Emma I want her to see.

Roger Fucking punt!

Emma Mr Boily's going to pop!

Roger Untie me, Emma.

Emma Emma can't do knots.

Roger That's childish, Emma.

He struggles with his ropes but has no success.

Please, Emma.

Emma You've got about forty-five seconds.

Roger Forty-five seconds.

Emma Make everything all right. This all right.

Pause.

Roger (*very fast*) Well. I think we have to look at things as a tube. A sort of tube. Like a toothpaste tube. Now, in order to survive, man, woman, has to employ reason. Reason is by definition good because it seeks the optimum conditions for survival. Those conditions are peace, co-operation and plenty. Now, as we know, man, woman, has a dark side, and that – here we have to give Freud due credit – is suppressed for the benefit of civilization. But this dark side sometimes has to be released in small quantities like toothpaste being squeezed from a bulging tube. So . . . so . . . this is what is squeezed out to relieve the pressure. And that must be a good thing. Ultimately reinforcing the very fabric of social cohesion.

Emma I didn't understand a word of that.

Roger Emma, it's very simple . . . a tube . . .

Emma Is that the sort of thing you tell your students? You make it up as you go along. No, Roger, no. It didn't work. I'm sorry. Tube or no tube look at us, what we've been doing. You can't make it decent or useful.

Roger (*very upset*) Emma, Emma, I don't know what's been happening to me. I'm frightened all the time. What have I been doing for the last ten years? I feel like I must have been asleep. Where have they gone? I feel like I've woken up and my life's just gone by and I never noticed. And what's ahead of me? A sort of blackness. I'm not really sleeping, I'm drinking. I'm scared, Emma, scared.

Emma is moved.

Emma Poor Roger.

Miranda's voice, off.

Miranda Hello!

Roger and Emma freeze. Then Emma grabs the blanket that covers the painting and flings it over Roger so that his ties cannot be seen.
Miranda enters.

Miranda Why are you all wrapped up?

Roger I was asleep, I was asleep and Emma came in.

Emma I brought the painting for you.

Miranda No luck?

Roger Don't let's go into all that.

Miranda I'm just asking.

Emma No. She didn't like it. So I thought you might like it. You're always going on about it.

68

Miranda I think it's wonderful, that's why. You can't just give up, Emma. It's so like you to give up after one try. Isn't it, Roger?

Roger No.

Emma Just leave me alone.

Miranda I'm only keeping on about it because I know how much support you need.

Roger Just leave her alone.

Miranda What's this? Some sort of conspiracy?

Roger No, no.

Miranda I just don't want you slipping back, Emma.

Emma Slipping back?

Miranda Yes.

Emma I haven't just slipped, Miranda, I've plunged.

Roger Stop!

Emma We both have.

She pulls blanket off Roger, revealing his ties.

Roger Christ. (*He falls off the sofa and begins to try to wriggle across the floor.*) Ah! (*He stops, jerks, shakes, goes unconscious.*)

Miranda Roger?

His ties are revealed. Miranda stares at him.

Emma Better get him some water. Quickly.

Miranda exits.
Emma begins to untie Roger.

Sorry, Roger. (*She struggles with ropes.*) I tied these a bit

69

tight. Maybe, maybe in a few years all this will have
blown over. Maybe, maybe then we can even be friends
again.

   Roger sighs.
    Miranda re-enters.

He's still breathing.

   Roger opens his eyes.

Roger Miranda?

Miranda Don't try to sit up.

Roger I'm okay. I'm okay.

Miranda You may have had a heart attack.

Roger No, no. I haven't.

Miranda I'll phone for an ambulance. Don't try to
move.

Roger I don't want an ambulance. (*He gets up.*)

Miranda What are you doing?

Roger I'm going to change. (*He exits.*)

Emma I can explain, Miranda.

Miranda Don't.

Emma But I want to. I think, right from the beginning,
from the very first time we met, we've been building up to
this. This moment.

Miranda I don't want to listen to this.

Emma I always looked up to you and wanted to be like
you. But I was different. You knew that but it made you
powerful to feel you had to help me. You were full of
theories and the right way to be and in the end it began

70

to feel like criticism. Then I secretly began to hate you. And that's why. With Roger.

Miranda I don't know you. Please go now.

Emma I'll wait with you. Make sure everything's okay.

Miranda No. Go.

Emma hesitates, then decides to go.

Emma I'll take the picture, shall I?

Miranda No. Leave the picture.

Roger comes back.

Emma Well, goodbye. (*She exits.*)

Roger It wasn't my heart.

Miranda What was it then?

Roger It's hard to explain. (*Pause.*) I think I was passing from one state into another.

Miranda What?

Roger Yes. A sort of shamanic process. Native Americans are very familiar with it.

Miranda Don't talk shit, Roger.

Roger Don't dismiss it, Miranda, you know nothing about it. We have parallels in our own culture. Illness. People get ill at times of traumatic change.

Miranda You shit. With my best friend.

Roger Look.

Miranda In that disgusting way.

Roger I am sorry. Truly sorry.

Miranda In my house. Did you ever think about me?

71

What it might do to me? Did you hate me too? Did you want to hurt me?

Roger No. No. That was the last thing I wanted to do.

Miranda I try. I try really hard. I work hard.

Roger I know. I know.

Miranda So why?

Roger I don't know.

Miranda You must know. There's always an answer.

Roger I don't know.

Miranda I'm still tired. I'm tired all the time, Roger. But I don't want to give in to it. And now this.

Roger I know. I know.

Miranda You prick.

Roger Miranda. Don't call me that.

Miranda Prick. You spineless prick.

Roger You have a fear of masculinity, Miranda.

Miranda Oh God.

Roger It's meant over the years that I have had to suppress certain male elements of my psyche.

Miranda No, no.

Roger Because I loved you and wanted to be with you, I have suppressed these elements but at a cost. A cost to me as a man.

Miranda You've done a bit of washing up. You've refrained from using the word cunt. You read *The Bell Jar*.

72

Roger I think there was a necessity in all that. It was an historical moment that I feel proud to have participated in but the moment has passed.

Miranda Nothing's passed.

Roger I think you've got stuck, Miranda. The world's moved on.

Miranda You've given up, Roger. That's all. Nothing's moved on. You've shrunk into the world of Roger. What's important to you is pleasuring yourself and when that get's boring and narrow you have to think up more and more perverse and degrading ways to do it. Will you be able to squeeze another drop of sensation out of your tired, sated body?

Roger You see, that's the thing. How you see me. But really I'm at a sort of peak. I have to start looking at myself dynamically. Being with people who look at me dynamically. As Alan said, I could still have children. A whole new start.

Miranda I'd hate to think I'd been holding you back.

Roger I'm going.

Miranda Going?

Roger To stay with Alan. He says there's plenty of room. (*Pause.*) Believe it or not I didn't plan all this. It just happened. I'll get my things.

Miranda You've settled for so little, Roger. How could you?

He exits. She is left alone. She calls after him.

How could you?

She puts the picture somewhere prominent and looks at it.

73

Paula and Miranda. Miranda's house. Around lie boxes.
Miranda is packing up Roger's things.

Paula It's urgent.

Miranda doesn't respond.

It's urgent, Miranda. I ran out. I ran out from work.

Miranda It's Sunday. Isn't it your day off?

Paula No. Wednesdays. I ran out. You have to phone
them, Miranda. I know I'm close to getting Victoria back.
Make some excuse. Just say something about social ser-
vices. I had an urgent appointment, something like that.

Miranda You explain to them, Paula.

Paula I can't. There's this cunt who's the manager and he
wants me on the night shift. I told him to fuck off and
then I came here. He can't do that, can he, Miranda?
What about Victoria? (*Pause.*) I think you should phone
him now. 407 4007. I have to go back. If you walk out of
a job you lose your benefits.

Miranda does so. It takes a lot of effort. Paula prompts
her.

Miranda Hello, I'm phoning about Paula . . . yes, yes.
Her social worker. Miranda Hurst. Yes, something came
up and I needed to see her.

Paula It's your fault.

Miranda It's my fault. Yes. I'm sorry. Very last moment.
Yes, of course . . . absolutely the last time. I'll explain
that, yes. (*She puts down the phone.*)

Paula Thanks. Are you moving?

Miranda It's my other half. He's moving out.

Paula Oh, sorry.

Miranda He'll probably want to come back soon. He's not a strong character.

Paula I can't imagine you with someone weak.

Miranda It was a mistake.

Paula I can't imagine you making a mistake.

Miranda I just hate seeing his things around. It's like being punched all the time. Well, you know what it's like. Getting someone out of your life.

Paula Smash something up.

Miranda Is that what you do?

Paula It helps.

Miranda You mean something like this. (*Pulls a disk out of a box.*) His book.

Paula Is it important?

Miranda He's been working on it for ten years.

Paula That'll do.

Miranda He'll have copies.

Paula It's symbolic, isn't it?

   Miranda puts it aside. Picks up a lone trainer.

Miranda I don't know what to do with this. It's just the one.

Paula Chuck it away.

Miranda You see, if I'm not careful, Paula, this is what's going to happen to me.

75

Paula What is?

Miranda Packed away. People would like to pack me away. They've tried to shrink me and that's because they want to make me scared to ask for things.

Paula Who?

Miranda But I'm not going to start thinking small. I'm going to start thinking bigger than ever.

Paula Oh.

Miranda Imagine, Paula. That you could be anything, anyone you wanted to be. Who would you be? What would you be? Imagine, Paula. Go on. Now.

Paula What?

Miranda Anything. Anything. Just imagine. (*Pause.*) All right. A scientist. I can see you as a scientist working with a team on a cure for leukaemia. You could help so many people. Children. Think of the gratitude of their parents. If you think about the human body, Paula, it's an incredible thing. The arteries, the veins reach into every part of us. And the blood itself breaks down into individual cells and each cell is a beautifully functioning system. And each of us has countless millions of them inside us. Perfect structures. Can you see yourself like that? That's how big we need think. That big.

Pause.

Paula So didn't Emma have any luck? The picture?

Miranda She didn't have immediate luck. But I know she could, Paula. If she wanted to keep trying. I've got a conviction about that.

Paula I better get back.

Miranda I'll see you next week, Paula. Same time as usual.

Paula leaves.
  Miranda treads on Roger's disk. Stands looking at the pieces.

SCENE SIX

The Hooded Man and Emma. Hooded Man hands Emma a cup of tea.

Hooded Man White, no sugar.

Emma Thanks.

Hooded Man I thought you seemed a bit different today.

Emma Different?

Hooded Man More sad, less angry.

Emma I almost killed someone the other day.

Hooded Man My God. Did you get carried away?

Emma He nearly did. In an ambulance. We thought it was his heart.

Hooded Man They do say it's important to eat a lot of fruit.

Emma It's just another thing to think about.

Hooded Man Tell me if I'm invading your privacy.

Emma All right.

Hooded Man So what do you do? For a living?

Emma I'm a failed artist.

Hooded Man Really?

Emma Yes.

Hooded Man Sketching?

Emma Sketching is involved.

Hooded Man Could you draw me?

Emma I can draw anything that sits still for long enough.

Hooded Man Draw me.

Emma Can you supply the paper?

The Hooded Man opens his briefcase and takes out pen and paper. Gives them to Emma.

Emma Well equipped as always.

Hooded Man That's what my wife always says.

Emma Aren't you going to take off the hood?

Hooded Man No, no. I want the hood.

Emma Please yourself.

Hooded Man Art's a hobby of mine, funnily enough.

They sit while she sketches.

Emma Talk to me.

Hooded Man What about?

Emma Why do you always wear a hood?

Hooded Man I enjoy it immensely.

Emma Why?

Hooded Man I just do.

Emma Can't you do better than that?

Hooded Man For you I can.

Emma Good. That's what I like to hear.

Hooded Man I like its darkness. I like being inside. Completely inside. Total enclosure. Nothing getting in. My own private world. Only children normally have that privilege. Is that satisfactory?

Emma It'll do. There.

Hooded Man That really is rather choice.

Emma Oh, thanks.

Hooded Man Can I have it?

Emma If you want.

Hooded Man How much?

Emma Oh, no. Really. You can keep it.

Hooded Man That is silly. Throwing yourself away like that. How much?

Emma You really want it?

Hooded Man Yes.

Emma What would you do if I tore it up?

Hooded Man I'd be most upset.

Emma Say, 'Please, Emma, don't tear it.'

Hooded Man Please, Emma, don't tear it.

Emma 'It's very precious.'

Hooded Man It's very precious.

Emma A hundred pounds.

Hooded Man Seventy-five.

Emma Done.

Hooded Man I know a lot of people. Only it's not an interpretive field. Just drawing what's there.

Emma I prefer that. Just what's there.

Hooded Man Do you work in any other materials?

SCENE SEVEN

The group room. Nicola follows Miranda in.

Nicola I was nervous. I did okay, I think. I answered all the questions.

Miranda Well done.

Nicola Thanks. God knows what I'll face when I get home. The end of the world probably. That's what he was predicting when I left. Still, I've done it now. I've done it. I can't believe it.

Miranda Yes, congratulations.

Nicola I could never have got through it without you.

Miranda It was your hard work.

Nicola I wanted to say thank you.

Miranda You've no need to.

Nicola Paula's outside. She's just finishing her cigarette.

Miranda Emma won't be coming.

Pause.

Nicola I do think 'poor Dad'. He's sort of stuck, isn't he? And I'm moving away from him. I'll leave him. I will come back and visit, but it's not the same, is it? He'll be alone. I always say to myself the things you told me. I'm not just there to take care of him. I have rights too. I'm a person. He always rows with me about what I'm doing. Psychology, sociology. Passports to inconsequentiality. But then the other day I told him. I know what I want to do. I want to do what Miranda does. What you do.

Paula enters. She launches in.

Paula This is what happened. I'm not proud. I saw Victoria last Wednesday week, didn't we, Nick? Anyway, Tuesday I get a letter. I thought, this is fucking ridiculous, my own daughter writing me a letter. 'I've got my passport photos done on Saturday.' Passport photos! I went to work, then something went snap in my mind. I took twenty quid from the till and told them to fucking forget it. I got the train down, then I take a cab to Victoria's school. March into her classroom. I can hear the teacher asking me things. I just take Victoria. We go to the station. Next thing the police come. They take Victoria off me. I shout. I swear at them. They put me in a car. I resist. I fall over getting pushed into the car. That's how I got my eye. (*She turns slightly to show her eye, which is bruised.*) On the bright side, there's no charges because everyone's being understanding and I won't be working nights because now I won't be working. How bad is it? How badly have I fucked up?

Miranda I don't think the group is the place to discuss it, do you?

Paula Nick doesn't mind.

Miranda Whether she minds or not isn't the point.

Paula What is the point?

Miranda We need to discuss it on a one-to-one basis.

Paula Just tell me. (*Pause.*) I lost my head. I didn't hurt anyone.

Miranda And the eye?

Paula Yes?

Miranda Your eye.

Paula My eye? Yes?

Miranda You knocked it?

Paula Getting into the car. Yes?

Miranda I have to be satisfied, totally satisfied that you can provide a safe home for your daughter.

Paula Yes?

Miranda Yes.

Paula So this is a question about Michael? (*Pause.*) So I've seen him again. It's not against the law just because you've got some idea in your head. I fell getting into the car.

Miranda I don't believe you.

Paula This is rubbish. Are you telling me who I can screw? I actually like to screw. I'm not Mother Teresa. What is it? Do you want to choose someone for me? In your partnership role? I know you'll go for the GCSEs but can I put in a plea for a nice cock?

Miranda It's a clear issue.

Paula It's not a clear issue though, is it? He's never touched Victoria. Only me. Sometimes. And other people, not you, might decide that that is not adequate reason to keep a child from her mother.

Miranda So it's acceptable for her to watch you being beaten.

Nicola Please don't fight.

Miranda You have to make a choice. Michael or Victoria.

Paula I don't have to choose.

Miranda Not choosing is choosing Michael.

Paula I tell you something, Miranda. What I have chosen. I've chosen not to have you. I don't want to see you. I don't want to talk to you. I want someone else. Someone more reasonable. More normal. With less hang-ups. Someone who'll see my side.

Miranda Do you think you'll find someone who's prepared to give you what you want, no questions asked? A different sort of social worker? That's not going to happen, Paula, you might as well wake up to that. Choose your daughter.

Paula I'm not letting you choose for me. Imagine a future, any future, as long as it's the same as yours, Miranda. I'd rather swallow poison.

Miranda What are you going to do, Paula? Go back to your shitty life? Prostituting yourself. Living with a bastard. Just existing from day to day, barely coping. You ought to be glad that I was prepared to take you on.

Paula You're a fucking disaster for me.

Nicola Please stop arguing. Please.

Paula The thing is, sometimes I ask him to hit me. I ask him because I prefer pain on the outside. I prefer it.

Miranda I think you're very confused.

Paula No.

Miranda You're a mess, Paula. A mess!

Paula gets out her razor. She makes a cut in her arm.

Nicola Don't, Paula.

Miranda Don't do that, Paula.

Paula I prefer this. I prefer it on the outside. That's better.

That's much, much better.

Nicola You're bleeding.

Paula It's just a cut.

Nicola She's bleeding.

Miranda Let me get something for your arm, Paula.

Paula No. I've got something in my bag. You get it, Nick.

Nicola gets Paula's bag.

Cloth.

Nicola hands Paula a cloth, which she holds against her arm.

You don't know me. What I feel. You imagine you do, Miranda, but you don't. You go home to your nice house and your nice money. You don't know what it's like in the real world.

Miranda I do know. I told people I'd been sick. That was the easiest thing to say. But to tell the truth I was exhausted in a different sort of way. (*Pause.*) I found a child. Quite a young child. It was dead. Starved actually. A bus ride from here. A neighbour let me in. I really couldn't believe what I was seeing. I mean, you hear about things. You read reports, but it doesn't prepare you. I remember standing in that room and just feeling my mind emptying. Till there was nothing. Just me and the child in the room. When I got closer to the child I saw there were little cuts on its body. Tiny cuts. Hundreds of tiny cuts. Like stitches, but cuts. You only take that much care if it affords you some satisfaction. You see, I can understand anger, I can forgive anger. But satisfaction? Isn't that pleasure? It took me a long time, a long time to get back to myself after that.

84

Nicola That's like a sign. Dad would say it was a sign.

Miranda No, no. It's not a sign.

Nicola What is it then?

Miranda What pulled me through was the thought that I was needed. Because if people stopped caring . . . (*She gathers up her stuff.*) I'm tired.

Nicola Where are you going?

Miranda I'm tired.

Nicola You can't go. I need to talk to you.

Miranda Talk to Paula. (*She exits.*)

Nicola She's gone. I always felt safe here.

Paula You don't need her, Nick. Better off without her. You can get on with your own life. (*She lights up.*)

Nicola And water will fall from the sky. Floods will bury us, darkness will come and God's light will fade from the world.

Paula watches her, a bit alarmed.

That's Dad. Not me.

Paula Oh. You had me going there a minute. I'll be back here Monday. Starting all over a-fucking-gain. You'll be all right though, Nick. Students. They have a brilliant time. All they do is drink and have sex and then when their exams come up they take lots of pills to stay awake and do the studying they've been too busy to do before. Fantastic.

Nicola You have to study hard nowadays. There's a lot of competition for jobs. And you have to work too. Because you can't live off your grant.

Paula Oh. Oh well. Good luck.

Nicola Yes. I suppose I will go.

Paula Course you'll go. You can't stay with your old man, he's a lunatic.

Nicola What am I going for though?

Paula Well, it's something to do, isn't it? You can get a job at the end of it.

Nicola I didn't just want a job. I wanted something. Something I wanted to do. I wanted to feel something. That I was doing something important. Special. I didn't just want to join up dots. A to B. With no feeling behind it. Do you know what I mean?

Paula I don't know. I've got a headache. You'll be all right, Nick. You'll be fine. You'll study. You'll be brilliant. Then you'll land some dossy job.

Nicola But I want something. Something.

Paula Like me. I want Michael and Victoria and a bit of money. Look at the fucking time. I'm meeting Michael. Fancy a drink?

Nicola No, no. I better get back.

Paula Another time, Nick. Keep in touch.

Nicola Yes. Yes. I'll turn the lights out.

Paula You'll be fucking brilliant, Nick, Honestly.

Paula exits. Nicola stands for a moment looking at the room. There is a bright flash of light, noise. Whether it is frightening, as in a thunderstorm, or hopeful, as in a bright future, is ambiguous. Nicky stands unsure.
Lights go down.

86